THE DICTIONARY DEFINES THE WORD 'CHEF' as one who cooks in a skilled or professional manner. I've been a personal chef since 2005 and know what it takes to meet the challenging needs of our clients. It's not always as easy as one would think. However, Chef Rome has mastered the art of providing topnotch service and he provides it to all clients, whether or not they have celebrity status. He has delivered remarkable quality, consistency, and unmatched professionalism.

These have become his quintessential trademarks. His southern-meets-gourmet cuisine has taken him around the world and inspired young chefs and everyday foodies alike. To that end, I applaud Chef Rome for his accomplishments.

To Chef Rome: thank you for giving me entree with the big fella. I hope to soon pay it forward. I wish you nothing but the best in every endeavor and know that extraordinary success is but a stone's throw away. As you continue to excel in the culinary world, mentor our youths, and strive to perfect your cuisine; I only ask that you continue to be a chef's chef.

Chef Alex Conant
Personal Chef to Shaquille O'Neal

GOD IS EVERYTHING. *Without Him, I am nothing. Because He is, I am. Heavenly father, I owe you everything. I pray that I represent You in a way that makes You smile when You look down on me. Thank You for the gift of feeding Your people well.*

To my son Joshua, know that all I do is for your future. You are my namesake and you mean everything to me. I love you and I'm thankful for the gift that you are to me. To my daughter, Jasmine, I will never forget the very first sandwich you ever made for me. That was a lot of mayo. You're my princess and my angel. I love you and your brother like my next breath. Daddy is always just a phone call away. Keep cooking. You're further along now with your cooking than I was at your age. I love you, beautiful. The two of you will forever be my inspiration.

I want to thank my attorney, Lindsey Maxwell. Thank you for keeping me straight and the haters off my back. To Karima Mariama-Arthur, my sister and friend, where have you been all of my life? I'm thankful to God that he has sent you my way. You're the spark that my company needed to make things happen. I thank you and am forever grateful. To Domenick Nati, my brother and friend, all I can say is thank you. You gave me wings and watched me take flight. I appreciate you more than you know. God bless you and your company forever. To Brenda Koplin, Tabby Simpson and Erica Jeffries, thank you all for your diligence and attention to detail. Your final efforts were truly the icing on the cake.

To my mother, Katherine, I love you. Thank you for not stopping me the morning that I burned those pancakes. To my father, Otis, I guess you can take credit for giving me this cooking gene. I know we go back and forth about who the better cook is between us. That question is well settled and I think we both know the answer to that. To all of my sisters, brothers, cousins, and friends, there are far too many of you to name; but I love you all. To Chef Tony Moore, my friend and brother; you are the best. I thank you from the bottom of my heart. Now get back to work.

To Tunda Wannamaker, Rosina England, and Kim McCrackin all I can say is thank you all for your divine words of inspiration and prayers.

To Byron Cage, Brevin Knight, Shaquille O'Neal, Raymond Felton, Mike Bibby, Kenyon Martin and every celebrity that trusted me in their kitchens. I thank all of you. You could have hired anyone else, but you chose me. I hope that I've touched your lives in a memorable and positive way. You are all a huge part of my overall success. I hope that one day I can bless someone else in the way each of you have blessed me. Savor the flavor!

A **NOTE**
FROM ROME

Our taste buds dance to a rhythm of delightful flavors of timeless recipes. There is nothing greater than the smiles that grace the faces of my ancestors, siblings, family, and friends.

It's amazing how the very presence of food can bring so much joy and fulfillment. It is because of this that I am humbled by the great gift that God saw fit to place within my hands.

As I have the opportunity to serve others, I realize that an unexplainable joy takes over me as the wisdom to create such a taste has blessed the lips of so many.

Through this book, I've shared with you the treasures of my visions, creations, and passion.

My friends, grab your aprons and let's make our way to the kitchen. Join me in spirit as we embark upon A FLAVORFUL JOURNEY!

It's amazing how the VERY PRESENCE of food can bring so much joy & FULFILLMENT.

TABLE OF CONTENTS

95 | FAMILY, FRIENDS & MY MOST REQUESTED DISHES

SOUPS, SALADS & DRESSINGS 120

DESSERTS 168

MY EARLY
YEARS

COOKING IS MY GIFT and I am grateful for it. Some of you may be familiar with the story of how my cooking journey began, but for those who are not, allow me to explain. One morning when I was only 7 years old, I sat in my mother's kitchen and watched her cook pancakes. I remember literally watching every step of what she did. Her pancakes were to-die-for: they had a rich, buttery flavor and edges that formed a perfect golden crust. The next morning when I got up, I went into the kitchen and began to do everything that I could remember my mother doing the morning prior.

I placed the cast iron skillet on the stove, turned on the gas flame, began to mix the batter, and finally poured it into the hot skillet. Evidently, my mother smelled the burnt pancakes cooking. She got out of her bed, rushed into the kitchen, and said, "Turn down the flame, it's too high." I'm still amazed at the fact that she didn't spank my behind. I also figured that since I didn't get into trouble for messing with the gas stove, I was doing something right. Sure, I hadn't done everything correctly that morning, but my mother seemed genuinely ok with it.

*I'm still **amazed** at the fact that* SHE DIDN'T SPANK MY BEHIND.

Before long, I began to cook at every available opportunity, with or without my mother's permission. The fact that I burned a lot of pancakes that morning was almost beside the point. My mother ate them as if I were the next Top Chef. Apparently, she saw something special in me and wanted to encourage me to develop my gift.

Many of the men on both sides of my family are great cooks. My father makes biscuits so light and fluffy that they seem to float. Indeed, my father is a wonderful cook. We have an ongoing playful battle about who the better cook is between us. The truth is that we both have tremendous passion for cooking and it shows.

My son Joshua also likes to cook and I have to give my father the credit for that influence. My brother Ken makes a mean BBQ sauce. My Uncle Larry makes the greatest hushpuppies

I've ever eaten. My Uncle Jimmy seems to make the best of everything he touches, and my cousin Junior Shorter makes the best ribs money can buy. As you might imagine, these men are constant reminders of generations of brilliant cooks. They continue to be an inspiration every time I go into the kitchen.

All of this doting on the men-folk certainly does not mean that the women in my family cannot cook. Nothing could be further from the truth. During the holidays at my Aunt Fredia's house in Orlando, delicious

Love and laughter always filled the space in celebration of our commitment to each other. No matter if a cousin lived right around the corner or six states over, the greetings were tremendous and heartfelt. I am blessed to have come from such a large family. Our grandparents blessed us with the great lessons of how to treat one another.

My grandparents had 23 children. Yes, 23 children from two people who loved one another dearly. That's not a typo. My mother is the oldest girl in the bunch. Obviously, I have many fond memories of

One of my *fondest* **memories** is of
MY **GRANDMOTHER** MAKING
BISCUITS *FROM SCRATCH.*
I can recall the smell of those biscuits as they baked in the oven.

food emerges as the focal point of every celebration. You can smell it cooking all night long!

My Aunt Bette can go into the kitchen and rouse aromas that get the whole neighborhood excited. My Aunt Brenda makes the best cakes and Aunt Bessie makes incredible macaroniand cheese.

I think we all have relatives who can make classic dishes with savoir-faire, right? This is exactly the point and precisely why I love to reflect on family gatherings. Often times we would meet at my Aunt Gladys's house in Rocky Mount, North Carolina.

my family. Amongst the most significant, however, is the fact that food always has, and always will, bring us together.

I was born and raised in East Orange, New Jersey, and almost every summer we would go down south. One of my fondest memories is of my grandmother making biscuits from scratch. I can recall the smell of those biscuits as they baked in the oven. I enjoyed them with honey, pear preserves, and even molasses on occasion. My grandfather was a sharecropper and made sure that there was always food on the table.

Even though my grandparents are no longer with us, they left behind some very important lessons. For example; how a family should come together to resolve any issues that it might face. My grandmother also left her biscuit recipe to each one of the girls. Over time, I have learned that it's not about the biscuits, pancakes, or anything else that my lovely family can cook. It's about having the right tools to bring families back around the dinner table. In our fast-paced society, everything has become hurried.

Remember the days when we sat around the dinner table and had simple discussions about our day? That's what good food does; it brings people and families together. Good food creates a great experience long remembered after the meal. Not surprisingly, I am not the only chef in my family. My cousins Edward and Travis are excellent chefs in their own right. We each serve in different niches within the culinary world and exchange stories about the vast differences between our respective industries.

We've learned that no matter what industry you are in, the common denominator is that we all wish to share an expression of love through food. Anyone who cooks a meal with love and good intentions will affect people in a positive, lasting way. After all, isn't that what it's all about?

I can go on for days talking about the cooks in my family. My point is that I realize that I come from a long line of great cooks and it's simply in my blood. It's what I do and love. By the time I turned 14, I could cook just about anything, but I wanted to take a break from cooking. I wanted to play sports. I'm a huge sports fan and since I was going to high school around this time,

that's what I decided to do. But two of my sisters, Amanda and Tricia, would come straight home from school, fix themselves a hearty snack, clean up after themselves, then wait for me to come home and would claim they were starving.

I've learned that people are funny. Some will do almost anything for a good meal. These two characters would feign the most famished looks. Later, I found out that it was merely a ruse so that I would cook. Now they want to take credit for my success by claiming they gave me the practice I needed to get this far. Although they are probably unwilling to admit it, they know that they used me for a good meal and that about sums it up!

Since the days of my youth I've had the ability to remember a dish and duplicate it in presentation and taste. Years can go by and I'll remember the taste of an extraordinary meal. My mother had a friend from Guyana who introduced us to curry chicken and roti. This still remains one of my favorite meals and its bevy of flavors is what I remember the most. I often take the taste of great dishes with me into every cooking situation.

18, and were immediately thrust into the rigors of the military. We had to assume responsibility for billions of dollars' worth of equipment, as well as for each other.

Dining facilities in the Army had regular meal hours just like any restaurant. Oftentimes I would see a young soldier running to get into the facility before the doors were locked. I had a choice. I could stand there and lock him out, giving him that "we're closed" wave, or I could let him in and give him my plate. If that were your son or daughter, what would you want me

Since the days of **my youth**
I'VE HAD THE ABILITY TO *REMEMBER A DISH*
& DUPLICATE IT
in presentation and taste.

Just about every job I have ever held involved food. I went into the United States Army as a cook at the age of 19. I have to be honest and say that I thought it was going to be easy and that's why I chose it.

Some would question why I chose the job for its simplicity rather than my own fervor. I would argue that the real passion came later or at least its revelation. Sure, I love to cook, but I love to eat even more. I ultimately realized my passion for cooking when I contemplated several events involving my fellow soldiers. As young as we were, we managed a great deal of responsibility. Many had just turned age

to do? Most days, I did it. I let him in. But, if he caught me on the wrong day, well, let's just say it's not what Jesus would have done. Two things are most important to the morale and sanity of a soldier: his money and his food.

We called it chow back then. Don't mess with a soldier's chow. Army chow was the best if you were in my dining facility. Every team of Army cooks that I had the pleasure of serving with were tops in the area. As a young private, I remember being stationed at Fort Carson, Colorado. My team won the Philip E. Connolly award for the best dining facility in the field. That says a lot considering you're competing against teams not only on your base, but also on other Army teams all over the United States.

Recently, I had the privilege of visiting Ft. Knox. It was like a homecoming of sorts. During my visit, however, I hardly recognized the rhythm of the base. I remembered as a young soldier in the Army, if you messed up, someone would make you work all day or an extra shift. When you consider the fact that on most days we would have to be at work at 4:00 a.m., no one wanted to work an extra anything.

I'll never forget the time when Sergeant First Class Sylvester Harrison walked through the doors of our dining facility. I was doing the unthinkable. I was hosing down a meat slicer with a water hose while it was still plugged in. I knew better, but I was so tired after that particular shift that I didn't care. I was being just plain old lazy. He took one look at me and said, "Soldier, if you worked for me, you would be working all day for the next 45 days." My response to that was "Well, I'm glad I don't work for you." Unfortunately for me, he turned out to be my next boss.

Needless to say, I was reminded of the meat slicer incident. That was the moment I realized the literal meaning of the "U.S. Army does more before 9:00 a.m. than most people do all day." I became a living example of those words after he was finished with me. That was one first impression that I wish I could've taken back. Fortunately, after being disciplined, I was given another chance to prove I was not the irresponsible soldier that he thought I was; but it took a while. Sergeant Harrison is now one of my closest friends. He's currently retired and living just outside of Ft. Bragg, North Carolina.

Everything is so different in the dining facilities now. They use far more advanced food prep equipment. Most of the workers are not Army cooks, but civilians. I'm not sure how much I like that. Nothing against the civilians, I just thought I was going to

My life has *changed* a lot since the DAYS OF **BURNT** PANCAKES & smoky **kitchens.**

see Army soldiers slicing and dicing fresh vegetables and following the military's technical manual to create recipes. But that was not the case. It seemed as though the Army had gone corporate. Either way, as long as our soldiers are being taken care of as they protect us from our enemies, both at home and abroad, that's all that matters.

My life has changed a lot since the days of burnt pancakes and smoky kitchens. I've gone from being a cook at Gardner's BBQ in Rocky Mount, North Carolina, to what many would call a celebrity chef. I've never considered myself a celebrity chef.

13

But, the media uttered it first and soon it just stuck. I don't know, sometimes it feels a little weird to me. Although I'm thankful for the notoriety that it brings, I just want to bless my clients with an expression of love through food. It's for this reason that I've written this cookbook.

I never had the privilege of going to culinary school. For a while, it was something that brought great shame. How dare I call myself a chef? I wondered who would respect my cuisine if I lacked the appropriate academic credentials. However, when I realized that this gift could take me from being a short order cook to commanding the attention of chefs from all over the world, compel celebrities to request assistance with weight management goals, and summon junior chefs to seek me as a mentor, I knew that this is what God intended. For everything that I am and all that I have achieved, God receives all the glory.

My passion for cooking continues to burn deep within. As I continue to cultivate this gift, I realize that I am fortunate to be in every kitchen in which I cook and have a unique responsibility to every client that I serve. It is mine to create a positive experience long after the meal is over. These recipes reflect the early days of my youth as I grew up in East Orange, New Jersey, and Warren, Ohio. They are equally symbolic of those moments that have made me the man that I am today. Bon appétit!

My passion **for cooking** *continues* **to**
BURN DEEP WITHIN.

UNCLE JIMMY'S **BBQ WINGS**

THERE'S NOTHING LIKE the food cooked by your favorite uncle. Every family has one. Some fry the best fish, or handle the big family cookout every year. And of course, there's the favorite rich uncle. (I don't have one of those.) In my family, my uncle Jimmy (we call him Raeford, don't ask me why) is one of several uncles of mine that can really burn in the kitchen. There's nothing like being home in Rocky Mount, North Carolina, when my family is cooking. This particular afternoon, I was standing on my uncle's porch waiting to go inside when the smell of his grill hit me square in my nostrils. I was on my cell phone at the time. I forgot what I was talking about. All I can remember saying was, "I'll call you back, I'll call you back." He was in there making his killer BBQ wings. So here is my rendition of what we ate that day.

(SERVES 4)

12 whole chicken wings
(washed well, removed of any remaining feathers, and patted dry)

¼ cup of olive oil

1 tablespoon of seasoned salt

1 tablespoon of ground black pepper

1 tablespoon of granulated garlic

½ cup of cider vinegar

½ tablespoon of red pepper flakes

½ cup of sugar

1 cup of ketchup

PREHEAT the grill over medium high.
PREHEAT the oven to 375 degrees.

DIRECTIONS

Season the wings with olive oil, seasoned salt, black pepper, and garlic. Place the wings on the preheated grill. Cook the wings until completely done. While the wings are cooking, place a medium-size pot on the stove over medium high heat. Add the vinegar,

DIRECTIONS (cont.)

pepper flakes, sugar and ketchup to the pot and bring to a boil. Stir constantly. Reduce the heat to medium low until the sauce thickens. Remove the wings from the grill and place into a roaster pan or sheet pan. Dip each wing into the sauce and return to the pan. Pour any leftover sauce over the wings. Cover the roaster or pan and place in the oven and bake for 30 minutes. This will allow the sauce to soak into the wings. Remove the wings from the oven and enjoy. Lick every finger as you enjoy!!!!

BRUNSWICK STEW

I DID A LITTLE RESEARCH on the origin of Brunswick stew. Chef Jimmy Mathews became a culinary genius when he came up with this recipe in 1828. One of the great things about coming from a long heritage of men who cook is that I get to hear all the stories of how recipes came about or how they evolved into a family favorite.

As my father grew up in Clayton, Alabama, his dad would make an awful lot of money from his neighbors by selling his homemade Brunswick stew. He recalled the days of standing there watching and helping out as needed. Back then the stew was cooked outside in the old-fashioned big black wash pot. It sat on three legs. The rocks aligned the outside of the pot creating an in-ground pit. He spoke about how the stew would cook for hours and hours. I'm told the aroma could be smelled a long way off. I've enjoyed my father's version of Brunswick stew and now I'll pass it on to you. You will need a Dutch oven or large soup pot to get started.

(SERVES 4)

2 whole chickens *(cut into parts)*

1 ½ pounds of pork shoulder

4 beef or veal soup shanks *(diced)*

Enough water to cover the meat

4 cans of tomato puree

1 can of tomato paste

2 cans of diced tomatoes

1 bottle of ketchup

2 cups of Worcestershire sauce

2 cups of frozen green lima beans

2 cups of whole kernel corn

1 can of creamed corn

1 cup of fresh cut green beans

½ cup of prepared mustard *from the jar*

1 tablespoon of cayenne pepper

2 cups of hot sauce

DIRECTIONS

Place the chickens, pork, and beef in the pot. Add enough water to cover the meat. Bring the meat to a boil. Cover the pot and reduce the heat to simmer. Allow the meat to cook for 2 hours. Remove all the bones and continue to cook until the meat has become tender. Add the remaining ingredients. Continue to simmer for 3 hours. Stir the pot every few minutes or so to prevent sticking.

One of the **great things about** coming from a
LONG HERITAGE
OF MEN **WHO COOK** *IS THAT*
I get to hear all the stories of
HOW RECIPES CAME ABOUT
or how they evolved into a **family favorite.**

SALMON CROQUETTES WITH PEPPER JACK GRITS

DIRECTIONS

Drain the canned salmon. Reserve ¼ cup of the liquid so that the croquettes don't become dry during the cooking process. Place the salmon and the ¼ cup liquid in a large bowl. Season the salmon with pepper, salt, lemon and garlic. Lightly toss the seasonings into the salmon. Sprinkle the flour over the salmon and add the egg. Toss lightly until the egg and flour are well incorporated. Place the bowl into the refrigerator for about 15 minutes. Place a large skillet onto the stove, and preheat over medium high for about 10 minutes.

Form the croquettes in your hand creating an oval shape. Lightly coat the croquettes in the corn meal. Add the oil to the pan. Place the croquettes immediately into the pan. Cook the patties for about 3½-4 minutes on each side. Drain the croquettes well on a paper towel. To prepare the grits, place a small pot on the stove. Bring the water, milk, and butter to a boil. Stir the grits into the pot. Cover the pot and reduce the heat to low. After 2 minutes, stir the grits to prevent

(SERVES 4)

SALMON CROQUETTES:

2 cans of salmon or mackerel

3 teaspoons of coarse black pepper

3 teaspoons of salt

Juice of ½ lemon

½ tablespoon of garlic powder

1 tablespoon of all-purpose flour

1 egg

½ cup of yellow corn meal

½ cup of vegetable oil

PEPPER JACK GRITS:

1 ½ cups of water

1 ½ cups of whole milk

1 stick of sweet cream butter

Pinch of salt

1 cup of quick grits

¼ cup of shredded pepper jack cheese

¼ cup of sharp Cheddar cheese

sticking. Remove the pot from the stove and stir in both cheeses. If my mother didn't make homemade biscuits, she would open a can of her favorite store-bought biscuits and serve them with this wonderful meal.

If my **mother** didn't make

HOMEMADE BISCUITS

she would **open** a can of her

FAVORITE STORE-BOUGHT BISCUITS

and serve them with this **wonderful meal.**

KATHERINE'S OVEN-SMOTHERED
CATFISH AND ONIONS

YEARS AGO MY MOTHER would make this dish. I just want to make you understand how the gravy from the fish would sink into the rice. OH MY GOD; it's really good! I was quite young when she cooked this particular dish, but I never forgot it. Of course my mother didn't believe in cooking anything that had alcohol in it. That was my own touch of culinary flair, if you will. Because my mother suffers from Alzheimer's, she hasn't cooked in years. However, I'll never forget the love that she gave to so many people through her cooking. I hope you enjoy this as much as I have over the years. This recipe will work any day of the week.

(SERVES 4)

1 ½ cups of vegetable oil

2 cups of all-purpose flour

2 tablespoons of garlic powder

2 tablespoons of coarse black pepper

2 tablespoons of salt

1 tablespoon of dry thyme

1 tablespoon of paprika

1 tablespoon of tarragon leaves

2 pounds of catfish fillets
*(washed and patted dry
with a paper towel)*

2 large Vidalia onions *(sliced)*

½ cup of white wine *(chardonnay)*

2 ½ cups of chicken broth

1 tablespoon of chopped parsley

PREHEAT the oven to 400 degrees.

DIRECTIONS

Place a large skillet on the stove on medium high heat. Pour the vegetable oil in the skillet and allow it to preheat for about 5 minutes. In a large bowl add the flour, garlic, pepper,

DIRECTIONS (cont.)

salt, thyme, paprika, and tarragon. Mix well. Coat the fillets in the flour mixture. Shake off the excess flour and place the fillets in the skillet. Cook the fish for about 3 minutes on each side. Remove the fish from the pan and place them in a casserole dish. Place the onions in the pan and sauté for about 3 minutes. Add the white wine and chicken broth to the skillet. Allow the broth to simmer for about 2 minutes. Pour the onions and broth over the fish. Cover the casserole dish with foil and place it in the oven. Cook for 45 minutes. Remove the casserole dish from the oven. Remove the foil and garnish fish with the parsley.

ROME'S
ORANGE ROUGHY
WITH PINEAPPLE SALSA

DIRECTIONS

Combine all the salsa ingredients in a small bowl. Mix well. Cover and refrigerate.

Preheat the oven to low broil. Apply nonstick spray to a sheet pan. Place the fillets on the pan and set the pan aside for later use. Using a clean coffee grinder, blend together the cumin, coriander, fennel seeds and cilantro. Grind to a fine powder. Pour the powder mix into a blender. Add the paprika, bell pepper, zest, orange juice, garlic, salt, and honey. Blend until smooth. While blending, pour a steady stream of olive oil into the blender. This will bring everything together. Use a pastry brush to apply the mixture over the fish. Place the pan in the oven and broil for about 6 minutes. Remove the pan from the oven. Spoon the salsa over the fish and serve.

(SERVES 4)

ORANGE ROUGHY

1 ½ pounds of orange roughy fillets *(rinsed in cold water and patted dry with a paper towel)*

1 tablespoon of cumin seeds

1 tablespoon of coriander seeds

1 tablespoon of fennel seeds

1 tablespoon of dried cilantro

1 tablespoon of ground paprika

1 orange and yellow bell pepper *(minced)*

Zest of 1 orange

Juice of 2 oranges

2 cloves of garlic

½ teaspoon of sea salt

3 tablespoons of honey

¼ cup of extra virgin olive oil

PINEAPPLE SALSA

2 cups of diced pineapples

2 tablespoons of rice wine vinegar

2 tablespoons of low sodium soy sauce

1 teaspoon of crushed red pepper flakes

¼ cup of chopped cilantro

Pinch of salt

SALMON FRITTERS
WITH APRICOT DIPPING SAUCE

DIRECTIONS

Preheat the oven to 350 degrees.

Season the salmon with the sesame oil, garlic, and pepper. Place the salmon onto the skewers and bake for 3 minutes on a lightly greased sheet pan in the oven. Remove the pan from the oven and set aside.

In a large bowl, sift together all the dry ingredients. Add the buttermilk, butter and vanilla. Stir well. Add the eggs and stir until well incorporated. Allow the batter to rest for about 5 minutes. While holding the wood end of the skewer, dip the salmon end into the batter. Immediately place the salmon end into the oil and deep fry until golden brown. Rotate the fritter to allow for even cooking. Cook for about 30 seconds. Place the fritters on paper towels to drain the oil well.

Place a large skillet on the stove on medium high heat. Add the butter and apricot to the pan. Allow the jam to dissolve. Mix well. Add the mustard, soy sauce, pepper flakes, and sesame oil. Allow the sauce to simmer

(SERVINGS WILL VARY)

SALMON FRITTERS

12-20 wood skewers
(soaked in water for 30 minutes)

2 pounds of fresh Atlantic salmon
(skin removed, washed and patted dry cut into strips about 1 inch wide)

½ cup of sesame oil

3 tablespoons of garlic powder

3 teaspoons of cayenne pepper

PANCAKE BATTER

1 ½ cups of all-purpose flour

3 tablespoons of sugar

1 ½ teaspoons of baking powder

½ teaspoon of salt

½ teaspoon of baking soda

1 ½ cups of buttermilk

3 tablespoons of unsalted melted butter

½ teaspoon of vanilla

2 large eggs *(beaten)*

(INGREDIENTS CONTINUE ON NEXT PAGE)

DIRECTIONS (cont.)

for about 2 minutes. Pour the sauce in a bowl for dipping. Arrange the fritters on a platter and enjoy.

APRICOT DIPPING SAUCE

½ cup of unsalted butter

½ cup of apricot jam or preserves

½ tablespoon of Dijon mustard

1 tablespoon of low sodium soy sauce

1 teaspoon of crushed red pepper flakes

½ tablespoon of sesame oil

BEEF **OXTAILS**

DIRECTIONS

Prep the oxtails by rinsing and trimming the majority of the fat off the larger pieces.

In a mixing bowl, combine the flour, salt, pepper and garlic powder. Mix well. Place a large skillet on the stove over medium high and preheat for about 4 minutes. Add the olive oil to the skillet.

Coat the oxtails in the seasoned flour mixture. Shake off the excess flour. Place the oxtails into the skillet. Brown the oxtails for about 2 minutes on each side. Do not overcrowd the pan. Repeat the process until all the oxtails are browned. Place the oxtails into a roaster. Add the thyme, onion, Worcestershire and enough beef broth to cover the oxtails.

Tightly cover the roaster with foil and place on the middle rack of the oven. Bake for 3 hours on 450 degrees. Reduce the heat to 350 degrees and cook for an additional hour. Serve over rice or mashed potatoes. Enjoy!

(SERVES 4)

3 pounds of fresh oxtails

2 cups of all-purpose flour

2 tablespoons of seasoned salt

1 ½ tablespoons of black pepper

2 tablespoons of garlic powder

1 ½ cups of olive oil

1 tablespoon of dry thyme flakes

1 medium onion *(chopped)*

1 ½ cups of Worcestershire sauce

6 cups of beef broth

PREHEAT the oven to 450 degrees.

BBQ LEG OF
VENISON
WITH COCA COLA SAUCE

DIRECTIONS

Most of the time fresh venison has a strong game taste. It is necessary to soak the meat in salt water, much like a cured Virginia ham. By adding salt to the water, this will not only draw out the strong game taste, but a lot of the extra blood as well. I recommend soaking for an hour submerged in the salt water.

Remove the venison from the water and place in a roaster. Make sure to drain the venison well and pat the venison dry. Preheat the grill on medium heat. While the grill is preheating, assemble the remaining ingredients for use. In a small bowl, combine the ingredients for the dry rub.

Apply to the meat liberally. (Make additional rub if necessary). Place the meat on the grill. Place the ingredients for basting in a small pot and stir well. Set aside until ready for use. Baste the meat every 15 minutes for a span of 1 hour.

Turn the meat after 30 minutes and repeat the basting process. Remove the venison from the grill and return to a clean roaster.

(SERVINGS VARY)

1 large leg of venison

½ cup of salt

DRY RUB

2 tablespoons of minced garlic

2 tablespoons of coarse black pepper

1 ½ tablespoons of seasoned salt

2 teaspoons of dry thyme

SAUCE FOR BASTING

1 cup of cider vinegar

½ cup of vegetable oil

1 ½ teaspoons of crushed red pepper

FINISHING SAUCE

2 cans of Coca Cola

1 tablespoon of rum flavor
(1 ½ oz. of spice rum, optional)

3 tablespoons of cooking sherry

1 stick of unsalted butter *(cold and sliced)*

Pour the remaining basting sauce over the meat. Cover with foil and place in the oven for 4 hours. Remove the roaster from the oven and allow the venison to rest. In the meantime, prepare the sauce.

SAUCE: Pour the Coca Cola, rum flavor, and sherry into a saucepan. Bring the sauce to a boil. Reduce the heat to simmer. Pour the sauce over the venison and continue to cook for 15 minutes. Turn the oven off and remove the venison from the oven. Place the venison on cutting board just before slicing and be sure to cut against the grain. Enjoy!

Most of the **time**
FRESH VENISON
has a **strong** game taste.

LOBSTER **COCKTAIL**

OVER THE PAST FOUR YEARS I've been fortunate enough to be invited back to Walt Disney World to participate in the Epcot food and wine festival. Each year I've done a live demo featuring some of my favorite signature dishes. I love a live show or demo. Nothing gets my blood going better than the energy from a hyped audience.

After my live demos, there's the Party for the senses. If you've never attended one of these parties, I'd say you owe it to yourself to do so. October 5th 2013 Chef Tony and I came up with a wonderful cocktail sauce like none other. Paired with grilled spiny lobster, we created one of the top dishes of the night, The Lobster Cocktail. This appetizer is great for entertaining. It's simple and can be prepared in advance. The seafood lovers thoroughly enjoyed this one.

(SERVES 8)

2 cans of tomato juice

4 roma tomatoes *(quartered)*

1 celery stalk *(small diced)*

2 cloves of garlic

1 small can of crushed pineapple *(drained well)*

1 small onion *(diced)*

1 tablespoon of prepared horseradish

pinch of salt

pinch of pepper

1 jalapeño pepper *(minced)*

½ cup of vodka

¼ cup of melted butter

2 pounds of lobster meat *(shells discarded)*

1 teaspoon of chopped cilantro

8 lime wedges or rosemary sprigs *for garnish*

DIRECTIONS

Place a 2 quart sauce pot on the stove over medium high heat. Pour the tomato juice into the pot. Add the tomatoes, celery, garlic, onion and pineapple into the pot. Bring

DIRECTIONS (cont.)

to a boil. Cover with a tight fitting lid and reduce the heat to simmer for about 45 minutes to an hour. Stir occasionally.

Remove the sauce from the stove and allow the sauce to cool completely. If you have a food processer or a great blender; puree the sauce until the mixture is smooth. About 10-15 seconds. Add the horseradish, salt, pepper, jalapeno, and vodka. Mix well. Adjust the flavors according to your likeness.

I prefer a little more heat. Perhaps a scotch bonnet or cayenne pepper will suit your taste buds.

Place the lobster on a preheated grill. Allow the lobster to cook for two minutes on each side. Remove the lobster from the grill and place on a cutting board. Cut the lobster into bite size pieces or chunks.

Place a skillet onto the stove over medium high heat. Add the butter and lobster to the skillet. Sauté the lobster for about 2 minutes. Sprinkle the lobster with the cilantro and splash of vodka (optional). Remove the skillet from the burner and allow the lobster to chill for about 10 minutes.

Fill the martini glasses half way with the cocktail sauce. Place 4-5 pieces of lobster in each glass and garnish with a lime wedge or your or a sprig of your favorite fresh herb. Edible flowers will make for a beautiful presentation as well. Enjoy the Disney magic we created on that night.

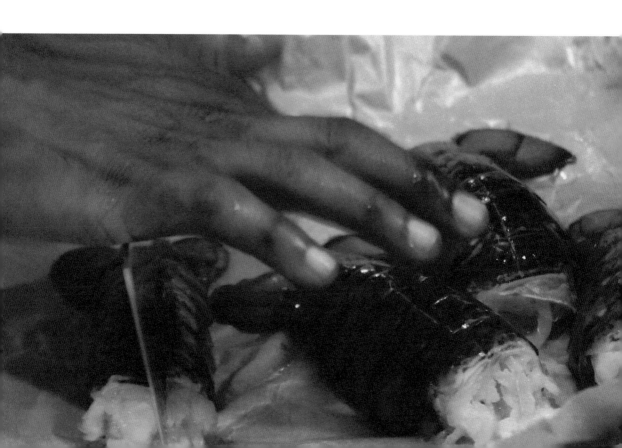

BONELESS
DUCK BREAST WITH
SZECHUAN PEACH SAUCE

DIRECTIONS

Season the duck breasts with the salt and pepper. (Set aside.)

Place a large skillet on the stove. Place the duck breasts in the skillet skin side down. Place the skillet over medium heat. Cook the duck breast for about 10 minutes until the majority of the fat has rendered or until the skin of the duck is crispy.

Turn the duck over and continue to cook for an additional 5 minutes or until an internal temperature of 125-130 is reached. Transfer the breasts to a platter and allow to rest. Drain the fat from the pan. (Reserve 3 tablespoons for later use.) To the pan add the sesame oil, peppercorns, red pepper flakes, garlic, ginger, scallions and brown sugar.

Sauté the seasonings for about 30 seconds, then add the soy sauce and peach juice. Allow the sauce to simmer for an additional 2 minutes. Pour the sauce over the duck. Add 3 tablespoons of duck fat to the pan. Add the peaches to the pan. Cook for 1 minute on each side. Remove the peaches from the pan and place on top of the duck as garnish.

(SERVES 8)

4 boneless duck breasts

4 teaspoons of salt

2 teaspoons of coarse black pepper

3 ½ tablespoons of sesame oil

2 tablespoons of Szechwan peppercorns

2 teaspoons of red pepper flakes

3 cloves of garlic

4 slices of peeled and chopped ginger

2 scallions cut into 2-inch pieces

2 tablespoons of brown sugar

3 tablespoons of low sodium soy sauce

½ cup of peach juice

1 cups of sliced peaches
(fresh or frozen, thawed)

CELEBRITIES **ATHLETES** &ENTERTAINERS

I'M OFTEN ASKED HOW I got started cooking for celebrities, athletes, and entertainers. I guess my response to that is, it was and is my destiny. I never set out to cook for any of these people; I just wanted to cook. While I was stationed at Ft. Drum, New York, I had the pleasure of working in a dining facility where I prepared a meal for the Chairman of the Joint Chiefs of Staff and the Secretary of Defense. In case you're wondering, those gentlemen were none other than General Colin Powell and former Vice-President Dick Cheney. Having those names on my résumé helped open doors after I got out of the Army.

It **was** & IS MY DESTINY.

I've always been an entrepreneur. While I was living in Raleigh, North Carolina, I started a company called 'Rent-A-Chef'. I was basically preparing dinners in private homes. It was good for a little extra money here and there. But, I had no clue about marketing and how to maximize profit. Eventually, I began making homemade cakes for the North Carolina State faculty club. I quickly found out that not only was I not charging enough for the cakes, I was also overworking myself. I was using my own gas and electricity, putting in crazy hours at home to meet the demand, and not being reimbursed for any of it. It didn't take long to figure out I needed to renegotiate the terms, or stop what I was doing. Needless to say, they already knew what was coming. Once I began to point these things out to the Executive Chef, he didn't seem so surprised. In fact, he wondered what took me so long to figure it out. That was my last day on that job.

One of the common things I experienced as a young chef was the inability to find a niche. I bounced around from one restaurant to the other; job after job, position after position. I worked at enough country clubs and hotels to remember almost every menu. Unfortunately, that didn't look very good on my résumé. It showed instability rather than expertise. I really needed to find something that I could stick with and since I didn't go to culinary school, I was simply learning as I went along. I lacked the basics to be able to compete with more seasoned chefs. My natural talent for cooking would only take me so far and what I had learned from the Army would only get me in the door. Benvenue Country Club in Rocky Mount, North Carolina, gave me plenty of gourmet experience, but it was insufficient to allow me to compete at higher levels. I worked there as a line cook. I made great soups and I learned quickly. But, what I really needed was to further develop my skills and experience.

In 1996 I got married and felt the need to do something greater than merely work for though I was there on a whim, I had a great feeling about the outcome. The interviews went well and I felt very confident about being given an offer.

I was feeling so confident that I returned to Raleigh and told my wife at the time to start applying for jobs in Orlando. It was a total leap of faith. We traveled back to Orlando while she interviewed for a couple of jobs in the area. By the time we got back, there was a message from Disney on our voice mail. The company arranged a follow-up call and another phone interview. A few

Even **though** I was
THERE **ON A WHIM**, I HAD A
GREAT FEELING
about the outcome.

someone else. We had our daughter a year later. So naturally, being a big dreamer, I set out on a course that would eventually change my life forever. I had always heard that if I could work for a company like Walt Disney World, the experience would catapult my career. I traveled to Orlando at my own expense and met with Disney's professional recruitment department. Talk about a busy place chockfull of diversity. All I could think about was working for Disney and making my mark in the culinary world. I saw Disney as the one place where it's magic and reputation could open up a world of opportunities. I was right. Even days later, I got the call that I had been waiting for. Disney not only hired me, but also moved my family to Orlando. Not much longer after that, my wife also received an offer for a prominent position in Orlando. I went ahead of my family to begin my new job and eventually my wife and daughter joined me. We bought a new house, and got settled quickly into our new surroundings. But soon things began to take a turn for the worse.

Not long after I started at Disney, my lack of experience began to show. Although I had management experience at different restaurants, and a solid military background as a cook, none of that prepared me for Disney's corporate structure. I must admit, I wasn't ready. I was written up more times than I can imagine for mishaps related to managerial duties. It wasn't the fault of Disney; it definitely trains its managers very well. Time management and punctuality were of the utmost importance, and consistency was a way of life. Notwithstanding, I failed miserably at these tasks and for these reasons, I was terminated. I learned some very valuable lessons from my experience at Disney. Getting fired was the best thing that could have happened to me and I am now a much better chef as a result.

Remarkably, no matter how hard I fall, I have always managed to get back up. I make learning from my mistakes a true priority and as a result, I have been blessed to continually land on my feet. Sometimes I meet young chefs who are headed down the wrong road, perhaps engaging in some of the same foolishness. My goal is to encourage them to raise their professional standards and develop thick skin. I advise that no one owes them anything, regardless of their education, experience, or skill level. Leave the attitude at the door. Remain humble, do your best, and always be on time. Remember to cook with passion and love. This advice has allowed me to suffer through my own setbacks.

After my tenure at Disney, I eventually took a job with the Central Florida Marine Institute, which is a great company that serves the Department of Juvenile Justice. While there, I taught life skills and served as a case manager for at-risk youth. These youth were in trouble and facing jail or even prison in some cases. I also had the

opportunity to teach basic cooking skills and provide them with a daily meal. For some, it was the only meal they would have that day. Many came from broken homes with one parent or in some cases, no parent at all. Some were actually raising themselves. I held this job for over a year. Eventually, one of the teachers introduced me to Isaac Austin's assistant; we called him Big Ike. At the time, Ike had just been traded to the Orlando Magic from the Los Angeles Clippers. I met his assistant at the BET soundstage at Disney of all places.

Two weeks after that meeting, I got the call from his assistant to come in for an interview.

The interview went very well. I was told that after a two-week trial period, a decision would be made whether or not to offer me the job. After cooking my first meal, I was hired on the spot. Ike was the very first professional athlete that I worked for as a personal chef. Working for Ike was an introduction to a new world. I had never known anyone who had that kind of money. I'd never seen so many diamonds, fancy houses, and cars. It was truly a new chapter in my life. Little did I know that this experience would serve as the training

income streams from a variety of directions; that's how you survive long after the cheers." Unfortunately for me, I began to get caught up in the routine. I was acting like Ike's life was my own and I had forgotten that I was there in my professional capacity.

I wasn't used to having unfettered access to women, money, and expensive alcohol. Thank God that I was never into drugs and neither were the athletes that I worked for. Regrettably, within six months of working for Ike, I was fired and too embarrassed to

Working **for Ike**
WAS AN *INTRODUCTION* TO A
NEW WORLD.

ground for the rest of my life. I had no idea what was in store, but would soon find out. One of the very first lessons that Mr. Austin taught me was to recognize my self-worth and maximize my potential.

As I was preparing his lunch one day, Ike said to me, "Jerome, its ok that you're my chef, but don't settle for that. Understand that I won't be in the NBA forever, and once my time ends, I can't continue to pay you the same type of salary." He told me to take advantage of my current situation and maximize the experience. "Create opportunities that will continue to bring

tell my wife why. Instead, I told her that because Ike had just been traded to the Washington Wizards, he was scaling back and wasn't taking me with him. I sunk into a deep depression that lasted for about seven months. I couldn't believe what I had done. All I could think about was how I had blown such a great opportunity. I was miserable. I tried to shake it off and apply for various others jobs, but it was all I could do to simply get through the day. I remember going into Dillard's Department Store to apply for a job. I had on shorts and some kind of wrinkled jersey. Needless to say, I didn't get the job.

After several months had passed, Ike paid someone to find me and we had lunch. By this time, I was separated from my wife and struggling to figure out my life. Thank God for second chances; I made the best of mine, too. In hindsight, I realize that the conversation that he and I had over lunch may have been the single most important conversation that we'd ever had. During our conversation, he'd offered the best advice I ever received from a client. Fast forward 13 NBA seasons. I've had the honor of cooking for many NBA athletes from Brevin Knight to Mike Bibby and Damon Jones to Shaquille O'Neal.

I've cooked for many athletes and each one has taught me a valuable lesson. I've always paid attention to the noble habits of each of my clients and of course certain things have just stuck. For example, Brevin Knight showed me how to manage money. He could have easily led a more extravagant life during his NBA career. He also took care of everyone around him first. He once told me, "Jerome, it's not what an individual asks for that's difficult to say yes or no to, it's who's asking that can create a difficult moment when I have to say no." That was good information!

Every morning as I would prepare Shaq's breakfast, he would sit at the counter and read the morning paper. By the time I placed his plate in front of him, he would have a good piece of investment advice. It's too bad I didn't have his kind of money to invest.

Byron Cage always spoke about the principle of giving. He'd say, "If you give freely, it comes back to you." I have to say that Byron is a living example of just that. These are examples that I strive to live by in my daily life. As I continue to

reach for a place of prominence within the culinary world, it is my intent to share these lessons. There is a lot of responsibility when someone has millions of dollars in the bank. The livelihood of some individuals depends on the work that they do for you.

> ## I've **cooked** for MANY **ATHLETES** &EACHONE has taught me a **valuable lesson.**

That being said, your bad day should not dictate how you treat your employees. I've seen firsthand how misplaced anger can cost someone a job. I've also seen how an employee's poor time management can ruin an employer's day.

The celebrity world is very different from the inside looking out. Most would never realize the kind of intense scrutiny under which celebrities live. When reviewing an interview with President Barack Obama on Super Bowl Sunday, he was asked about what it's like to be hated by some people.

I love what the President said. He said, "Those who hate me are those who don't know me personally." I thought to myself, that's exactly how those that I have worked for must feel. Our President spoke of the need to have thick skin to be the person that he is. Guess what? That's what it's like to be a personal chef. There's a need to have thick skin.

While I was cooking for Shaq, I had a day from hell that I quickly tried to forget. It was Thanksgiving Day 2005. I remember how

pick up the pieces and move on." I've been living by that advice ever since. By the way, my macaroni and cheese has been on point from that day forward.

Being a personal chef is better suited for a single person, especially if you have clients who are professional athletes. Their job locations can change from one moment to the next. I remember working for one athlete who was traded three times in one summer. Fortunately, I was able to remain stationary while that wild summer worked

While I was **cooking**
FOR SHAQ,
I HAD A **DAY FROM HELL**
that I quickly tried to forget.

my macaroni and cheese would not come out right to save my life. I must have made macaroni and cheese a million times, it seems, but this particular day it didn't work. I was devastated that such a simple dish had me stumped and caused dinner to be late. I could see the irritation on Shaquille's face.

That fact alone was very unsettling. However, he must have also seen how it was bothering me, so later that afternoon he came to me and said "Jerome, when you're the best at what you do, everything is under the microscope. Nothing escapes the eyes of those you cater to; suck it up, develop a short memory for the mistake,

itself out. When I initially became a personal chef to professional athletes and entertainers, I was married with two very young children. My marriage was on the rocks, and I was truly trying to find my niche in the culinary world. As I reflect on the various jobs that I've had, I realize that becoming a personal chef was exactly what I had been looking for. I had no one to manage but myself. I was able to further develop my creative talents and share the results with my clients.

I've also been fortunate to have clients with diverse palates. I could create with spontaneity and present dishes in a way that was pleasing to the eye as well as to the palate. Additionally, one of the things I enjoyed most about working with celebrities was their unique personalities. Shaq is a very funny guy. The public only gets to see a small amount of his big personality. I was able to experience it on a daily basis. One of the things that have always seemed to amaze people about me is the fact that I'm allergic to bananas. I can recall the day that Shaq asked me to make him a banana pudding. I told him that I couldn't because I have a banana allergy. You can only imagine the look on his face when I told him that. First of all, I'm telling this 7'1" mass of a boss, weighing in at 320 pounds that he can't have something that he's asking for. His reply to that was comical. He said "You're the only person I know that can be held up at banana point." I thought his response was funny as hell, but he was serious.

Needless to say, I found a way to get him a homemade banana pudding. My father lives in Orlando and since we were also in Orlando at the time, I was able to call him up and ask him to make it, to which he agreed. Shaq got his banana pudding and loved it. The only problem after that was Shaq suggested that he should fire me and hire my dad. I knew that my dad would have turned the job down anyway, so I wasn't worried.

As my journey takes me to a place of potential celebrity status in the culinary world, I'm reminded of why entertainers are so guarded about their personal lives. I learned very quickly why. It's awfully hard to live under public scrutiny. People don't want to be disappointed by their heroes. That's essentially what it amounts to. Our basketball stars, comedians, politicians, entertainers, and leaders are admired by the masses.

Behind closed doors, these public figures desire to be as normal as anyone else. They want to make a mistake and not be crucified for it. With so many fingers pointing in their direction, it's no wonder more celebrities don't simply lose their minds. Many question why celebrities should be given breaks since they have so much money and an apparently easy life. My answer to that is simple. The general public has no idea what it's really like. Being a public figure carries great responsibility. The late Biggie Smalls said it best when he sang the lyrics "More money, more problems."

The general public is essentially unaware of the responsibilities of being "rich." Many hands are outstretched. Extortion is very common. Scam artists come in all shapes, sizes, and colors. If you think its easy being rich, you might want to do your research first. Many of these celebrities wish they could be so-called "normal." Some wish that they could go back to the way things were before they became famous. If you ask me, I would say "give me the money and you keep the fame."

I'm thankful to every celebrity that I've ever worked for because each has given me an invaluable caliber of experience that has positively impacted my journey. As a result, I have raised my standards and further developed my culinary acumen. I take my hat off to each of you, and again I say thank you.

I take my hat off **to each of you, *and again***
I SAY THANK YOU.

BREVIN'S
FAVORITE ROAST

BREVIN KNIGHT WAS MORE than just another tremendous NBA athlete. I consider him and his family to be true friends. He's also an inspiration. I can recall making this roast for him and his family many times. I remember one occasion when I had to tell him "There is no more roast" and then watching this sick look on his face as if to say, "What do you mean there is no more?" I truly enjoyed being Brevin's chef and I will always cherish being his friend.

(SERVES 6)

2-3 pound chuck roast

2 cups of all-purpose flour
(after seasonings are added, reserve half for later use)

1 tablespoon of salt

1 tablespoon of coarse ground pepper

¾ cup of extra virgin olive oil

2 medium onions *(quartered)*

4 sprigs of fresh rosemary

4 sprigs of fresh thyme

8 cloves of fresh garlic *(crushed)*

½ cup of Worcestershire sauce

½ cup of low sodium soy sauce

8 cups of beef broth

DIRECTIONS

Place a large heavy-duty pot on the stove over medium high heat. In a medium-sized mixing bowl combine the flour, salt, and pepper. Coat the roast in the flour mixture. Pour the olive oil into the pot. Shake off the excess flour and immediately place the roast in the pot. Brown the roast for 4 minutes on each side.

Toss the onions into the pot with the rosemary, thyme, garlic, Worcestershire sauce, soy sauce, and beef broth. Bring the mixture to a boil. Cover the pot with a tight-fitting lid and

DIRECTIONS (cont.)

reduce the heat to low. Cook the roast for 2 ½ - 3 hours or until fork tender. Once the roast is tender, transfer the roast to a platter to rest for about 10 minutes.

In a small bowl, add ¾ cup of water to the leftover flour to create a smooth paste. Mix well. Return the broth to a boil. While stirring with a wire whip, add the flour paste to the pot until the gravy thickens. Slice the roast against the grain. Return the sliced roast to the gravy and allow it to simmer for 10 minutes more. Serve over rice or mashed potatoes.

BYRON'S
STEWED FLOUNDER

I'VE BEEN A PERSONAL CHEF to a number of athletes and entertainers. I have to say that of everyone I've served as personal chef, Byron Cage is the most inspirational to date. He truly appreciates good food and fine cuisine. We were in Washington, D.C., one evening as I began to prepare dinner. I learned very quickly that Byron loves seafood. I believe it's his food passion. During the course of his two-month diet program, I prepared a lot of seafood, but this particular recipe became his favorite. I called it stewed flounder. I hope you enjoy this dish as much as he does.

DIRECTIONS

Season each fillet with salt, pepper, and garlic. Set aside for later use. Place a large skillet on the stove and preheat over medium high heat. Pour the olive oil in the skillet. Add the shallot, bell pepper, and garlic. Sauté for two minutes. Add the tomatoes, tomato sauce, bay seasoning, clam juice, cooking wine, sugar, oregano,

(SERVES 2)

8 flounder fillets

Salt and pepper to taste

1 tablespoon of garlic powder

1 ½ tablespoons of extra virgin olive oil

1 shallot *(chopped)*

½ green bell pepper *(chopped)*

1 tablespoon of minced garlic

4 roma tomatoes *(diced)*

1 can of tomato sauce

1 tablespoon of bay seasoning

½ cup of clam juice

½ cup of white cooking wine

1 tablespoon of sugar

1 tablespoon of fresh oregano *(chopped)*

1 tablespoon of fresh basil *(chopped)*

1 teaspoon of dry thyme

1 teaspoon of cayenne pepper

2 tablespoons of fresh chopped parsley

DIRECTIONS (cont.)

basil, thyme, and cayenne pepper. Reduce the heat and simmer for 5 minutes.

Pour the sauce into a blender. Puree the sauce until smooth. Return the sauce to the skillet. Fold each fillet twice. Carefully place the fillets into the skillet. Cover the skillet and cook the fish for 4 minutes.

Place your favorite pasta or rice in the center of the plate. Arrange the fillets around the pasta. Spoon the sauce over each fillet. Garnish with fresh parsley and serve immediately.

I have to say that
of everyone I've served as personal chef,

BYRON CAGE

IS THE MOST **INSPIRATIONAL** TO DATE.

IKE AUSTIN'S SOUTHWESTERN GRILLED HALIBUT

I'VE COOKED FOR MANY NBA players and their families, but the one that I will always remember the most is Big Isaac (Ike) Austin. Ike was the first NBA athlete to give me the opportunity to be a personal chef. For that, I am forever grateful. Because of Ike's diverse palate, I not only improved my skills as a chef, but I was also free to be as creative as I wanted to be. Ike loves seafood, so the very first time I prepared grilled halibut, I had no clue that halibut was his favorite fish. Thank God it came out to his liking. Over the four years I worked for Ike, I must have prepared halibut over 100 ways. I believe you will enjoy this as well.

DIRECTIONS

Spray the grill with nonstick cooking spray. Preheat the grill for about 20 minutes before use. Rinse the halibut steaks and set aside. In a medium size bowl, combine the seasoned salt, chili powder, paprika, cumin, garlic, onion powder, cayenne pepper, and ground pepper. Mix well and set aside. Lightly brush the olive oil on

(SERVES 4)

Nonstick cooking spray

4 six-ounce halibut steaks
(about 1 ½ inch thick)

1 tablespoon of seasoned salt

1 tablespoon of chili powder

1 ½ teaspoons of paprika

1 ½ teaspoons of ground cumin

1 ½ teaspoons of granulated garlic

1 ½ teaspoons of onion powder

2 teaspoons of cayenne pepper

1 teaspoon of ground pepper

½ cup of extra virgin olive oil
(divided in half)

1 red, bell pepper *(sliced into strips)*

1 orange bell pepper *(sliced into strips)*

1 yellow bell pepper *(sliced into strips)*

1 ½ tablespoons of capers

½ cup of white wine

Juice of 1 lime

½ stick of unsalted butter *(slices)*

DIRECTIONS

both sides of each steak. Coat each steak with the spice mixture and place them on the grill. Cook for about 5 minutes on each side. Remove the steaks from the grill onto a sheet pan. Cover to keep warm.

Place a skillet on the stove over medium high heat. Add the remaining olive oil to the skillet. Add the bell peppers and capers; sauté the vegetables for about 1 minute. Add the wine and lime juice while continuing to cook. Simmer for about 2 minutes. Turn off the heat. Add the butter to the sauce one slice at a time. Allow each slice of butter to melt entirely before adding the next slice. Once all the butter is totally incorporated, pour the sauce over the halibut and serve immediately.

Over the **four years** I worked
FOR IKE
I must have **prepared halibut**
OVER 100 WAYS.

ITALIAN
BRUSSELS SPROUTS

I'VE NEVER MEET ANYONE who loves Brussels sprouts more than Byron Cage. I've certainly had clients who will eat the same thing every single day. For example, Mike Bibby will eat mashed potatoes every day. Shaq will eat a chicken leg quarter every day. Brevin Knight will have cranberry juice with every meal. It's almost a personal chef's nightmare. I wanted to come up with something that would not only give the Brussels sprouts a different flavor, but allow this under-used vegetable to have a new presentation. For those of you who are not fans of this great vegetable, I invite you to try it a new way. For those of you who already enjoy this wonderful vegetable, I invite you to try it this way. It's one of my favorite side items.

(SERVES 2)

Nonstick cooking spray

15-20 brussel sprouts
(rinsed and split in half)

2 teaspoons of seasoned salt

2 teaspoons of garlic powder

2 teaspoons of Italian seasoning

1 teaspoon of coarse black pepper

1 tablespoon of unsalted butter

½ tablespoon of olive oil

½ cup of Italian bread crumbs

¼ cup of Parmesan cheese

DIRECTIONS

Place a small pot of water on the stove (about 8 cups). Bring the water to a boil. Add the Brussels sprouts to the boiling water and allow them to cook for about 3 minutes. Drain the water from the sprouts and place them to iced cold water. (This will stop the cooking process and allow the Brussels sprouts to maintain their bright color. Once the sprouts have chilled completely, drain the water off the sprouts.

DIRECTIONS (cont.)

Season the sprouts with the salt, garlic, Italian seasoning, and pepper. Place a large skillet on the stove over medium high. Add the butter and olive oil to the pan and allow the butter to melt. Toss the Brussels sprouts into the bread crumbs. Place the Brussels sprouts in the skillet. Brown the vegetables on both sides for about 30 seconds. Sprinkle with Parmesan cheese and serve immediately.

For those of you **who are not fans** of this

GREAT VEGETABLE

I invite you to

TRY IT A **NEW WAY.**

SEAFOOD QUICHE

DIRECTIONS

In a large bowl, combine the flour and salt. Mix well. Press the butter into the flour with your hand. The flour should feel like course cornmeal. Mix the eggs and the water together. Add the egg mixture to the flour. Using a wooden spoon, mix well until the dough forms a ball. Divide the dough in half. Wrap the dough in plastic and place in the refrigerator for at least an hour before use. Roll the dough out. Allow the dough to rest. Shape the dough into the pie pans. Use a fork to prick the dough all over. This will prevent the dough from rising in the pan and will keep its shape. Bake at 375 degrees for 8 minutes. Remove the pie shells from the oven and cool for at least 10 minutes.

Place a large skillet on the stove on medium high. Add the butter and oil to the skillet. Sauté the lobster and crab for about 2 minutes. Season the lobster and crab with the bay seasoning. Add the broccoli, bell pepper and mushrooms to the pan. Continue to sauté for 2 minutes.

(MAKES 2 PIES)

DOUGH

3 cups of all-purpose flour

½ teaspoon of salt

2 sticks of unsalted butter *(soft)*

2 eggs

10 tablespoons of cold water

2 nine-inch pie pans

FILLING

2 tablespoons of unsalted butter

1 tablespoon of olive oil

4 ounce lobster tail *(chopped)*

8 ounces of lump crab meat

½ tablespoon of old bay seasoning

½ cup of chopped broccoli crowns

1 small red bell pepper

½ cup baby portabella mushrooms *(chopped)*

2 cups of sharp cheddar cheese

(INGREDIENTS CONTINUE ON NEXT PAGE)

DIRECTIONS (cont.)

Remove the skillet from the heat and divide the filling between the 2 pie shells. Divide the cheese between the two shells. Divide the egg mixture evenly between the two shells. Bake the quiche at 375 degrees for 45 minutes or until the center is set. Remove the quiche and cool for about 15 minutes. Cut into 8 slices.

8 eggs

2 ½ cups of cream

½ cup of half and half

HUNAN
CHICKEN

DIRECTIONS

Cook the noodles according to the directions on the package. Drain the noodles and set aside for serving. Place a large wok on the stove on medium high. Add the sesame oil to the pan, sauté the chicken breast and thighs for about 4 minutes. Add the broccoli, bokchoy, ginger, garlic, pepper flakes, black pepper, and cilantro.

Continue cooking for 2 minutes. Add the bell peppers. Combine the soy sauce, vinegar, and brown sugar. Mix well. Add the soy sauce mixture to the wok. Toss everything together. Spoon the noodles into bowls or on plates. Spoon the chicken and vegetable mixture over the noodles and serve immediately.

(SERVES 4)

1 package of Shanghai noodles

¼ cup of sesame oil

3 boneless skinless chicken breast tenders
(cut into bite-size pieces)

1 cup of broccoli crowns

4 baby bokchoy cabbages *(halved lengthwise)*

1 teaspoon of fresh ginger *(minced)*

4 cloves of crushed garlic

1 teaspoon of crushed red pepper flakes

2 teaspoons of coarse black pepper

2 tablespoons of chopped cilantro

1 large red bell pepper *(cut into strips)*

1 large green bell pepper *(cut into strips)*

1 large yellow bell pepper *(cut into strips)*

3 tablespoons of soy sauce

1 ½ tablespoons of rice vinegar

1 tablespoon of brown sugar

CASSOULET

DIRECTIONS

In a large bowl, cover the beans with the water. Soak the beans for 12 hours. Drain the beans in a strainer. Pour the beans into a large pot and cover with 10 cups of water. Cook the beans for about an hour or until they are tender.

Place a Dutch oven on the stove on medium heat. Place the bacon in the pan and cook until crispy. Remove the bacon from the pan but leave the fat. Place the bacon on a paper towel to drain. Add the sausage, chicken, onions, garlic, thyme, and bay leaf. Brown the chicken and sausage for about 10 minutes. Pour in the white wine, tomato sauce and 8 cups of chicken broth. Bring the pot to a boil.

Cover and reduce the heat to medium low. Simmer for about 40 minutes. Remove the bones from the pot and discard. Cover and continue to cook until the chicken is done. Spoon the beans into the Dutch oven and continue to cook for 10 minutes. Add the spinach and parsley to the pot. Ladle the Cassoulet into bowls and top with the bacon. Serve with sliced French bread.

(SERVES 6-8)

1 pound of great northern beans

8 ½ cups of water

4 strips of country bacon *(thick cut, diced)*

4 Italian sausage links *(cut into 1-inch slices)*

1 whole chicken *(cut up)*

1 cup of chopped white onions

2 tablespoons of chopped garlic

1 tablespoon of dry thyme

1 bay leaf

½ cup of white wine *(chardonnay)*

1 can of tomato sauce

10 cups of chicken broth

Salt and pepper to taste

2 cups of fresh spinach leaves

3 tablespoons of chopped parsley

THAI
TILAPIA

DIRECTIONS

In a blender, place the lime juice, fish sauce, brown sugar, vinegar, pepper flakes, mint, cilantro, garlic, and soy sauce. Blend for about 10 seconds. Set aside for later use.

Place a large skillet on the stove and preheat over medium. In a medium size bowl, combine the flour, salt, and pepper. Mix well. Add the olive oil and the butter to the skillet. Place the fish in the flour and coat each fillet well. Immediately add the fillets to the oil. Brown the fillets for 3 minutes on both sides. Pour the sauce over the fish and cover the skillet with a lid. Continue to let the fish simmer for about 2 minutes. I recommend this dish be served over jasmine rice.

(SERVES 4)

THAI SAUCE

¼ cup of lime juice

2 tablespoons of fish sauce

4 tablespoons of brown sugar

¾ cup of rice wine vinegar

3 teaspoons of red pepper flakes

1 tablespoon of chopped mint leaves

1 tablespoon of chopped cilantro

1½ tablespoons of chopped garlic

⅓ cup of low sodium soy sauce

TILAPIA

4 large tilapia fillets
(gently rinsed with cold water and drained well)

1 cup of all-purpose flour

½ tablespoon of salt

½ tablespoon of black pepper

2 tablespoons of extra virgin olive oil

2 tablespoons of unsalted butter

FIESTA SALAD FEATURING SHRIMP, STEAK, & CHICKEN

DIRECTIONS

Wash and prepare the romaine lettuce. Divide the lettuce between two plates and place them in the refrigerator to chill. In a small bowl, combine the cumin, chili powder, garlic powder, onion powder, cilantro and zest. Mix well. In individual bowls, season the shrimp, steak, and chicken with the spice mix.

Place a large skillet on the stove over medium high. Pour the olive oil into the pan. Sauté the shrimp, steak and chicken individually. Once the shrimp, steak, and chicken are cooked, combine all three in a bowl and toss with the tomato, corn, beans, cucumber, and lime juice. Divide the shrimp, steak, and chicken equally over the romaine lettuce. Top with the cheese. I recommend this salad with my **Southwestern Dressing.**

(SERVES 2)

2 cups of romaine lettuce
(chopped or shredded)

½ cup of salad shrimp *(washed and drained)*

1 six-ounce steak (rib eye, strip, or flank)
(sliced thin as for stir fry)

1 largeboneless skinless chicken breast
(cut into strips)

1 tablespoon of ground cumin

1 tablespoon of chili powder

1 tablespoon of garlic powder

1 tablespoon of onion powder

1 tablespoon of chopped cilantro

Zest of 1 lime

⅓ cup of extra virgin olive oil

1 medium tomato *(diced)*

½ cup of whole kernel corn

½ cup of canned black beans
(rinsed and drained well)

½ cup of diced cucumber *(peeled)*

Juice of 1 lime

½ cup of feta cheese

SOUTHWESTERN
SALAD DRESSING

DIRECTIONS

Combine all the ingredients in a blender or food processor. Mix well for about 15 seconds.

(SERVES 2)

2 large tomatoes (diced)

1 pinch of salt

Zest of 1 lime

1 tablespoon of paprika

Juice of 1 lime

1 tablespoon of chili powder

1 tablespoon of garlic (chopped)

1 tablespoon of cumin

¾ cup of red wine vinegar

1 tablespoon of sugar

1 tablespoon of chopped cilantro

1 shallot (chopped)

½ cup of extra virgin olive oil

SESAME BEEF,
ORANGE AND BROCCOLI

DIRECTIONS

Place a wok on the stove over high heat. Pour the sesame oil into the pan. Add the flank steak, garlic, ginger, pepper, thyme, and brown sugar. Sauté for about 5 minutes. Add the broccoli and toss.

Cover and continue to cook for an additional 3 minutes. Add the orange juice, hoisin sauce, oyster sauce, and juice from the mandarin oranges. Simmer for 2 minutes while continuing to toss well. Spoon the beef and broccoli onto warm plates.

Garnish with mandarin orange and sesame seeds. I love this dish as is or with Asian noodles.

(SERVES 2)

2 tablespoons of sesame oil

1½ pounds of flank steak
(sliced thin on an angle)

1 tablespoon of minced garlic

½ tablespoon of fresh ginger *(minced)*

½ tablespoon of black pepper

1 teaspoon of dry thyme

1 tablespoon of brown sugar

2 cups of fresh broccoli crowns

¼ cup of orange juice

1 tablespoon of hoisin sauce

1 tablespoon of oyster sauce

1 large can of mandarin orange
*(pour the juice into the pan
with the beef and broccoli)*

1 tablespoon of sesame seeds

HERB-CRUSTED BEEF
WITH MANDARIN
ORANGE MARMALADE

DIRECTIONS

Combine the herbs and chop well. Remove any large stems. Apply the mustard liberally to the beef. Add the herbs, pepper and salt. Wrap the beef in plastic and refrigerate for about an hour. Grill over medium high heat or broil in the oven until desired temperatures are reached.

While the beef is cooking, prepare the marmalade according to the directions below. Remove the beef from the grill and allow it to rest for about 5 to 6 minutes before slicing. Slice the beef at desired thickness. Cover and keep the beef warm.

Place a saucepan on the stove over medium high heat. Melt the butter in the pan. Add the onion, thyme, peppers, sugar, and vinegar, and sauté for about 3 minutes.

Add the remaining ingredients and continue to cook until the marmalade

(SERVES 2)

BEEF

Beef tenderloin
  (cleaned and silver skin removed)

¼ cup of basil *(chopped)*

¼ cup of thyme *(chopped)*

¼ cup of oregano *(chopped)*

¼ cup of rosemary *(chopped)*

3 tablespoons of garlic *(chopped)*

½ cup of Dijon mustard

2 tablespoons of cracked black pepper

2 tablespoons of kosher salt

MARMALADE

2 tablespoons of butter (unsalted)

1 large Vidalia onion (chopped)

1 tablespoon of thyme

1 teaspoon of black pepper

1 teaspoon of crushed red pepper flakes

¼ cup of sugar

(INGREDIENTS CONTINUE ON NEXT PAGE)

DIRECTIONS (cont.)

thickened. This should take about 5 minutes. Spoon the marmalade over the beef and serve immediately.

2 tablespoons of rice vinegar

Zest of 1 orange

Juice of 1 orange

2 cups of mandarin oranges

ROCK SHRIMP
POT PIE

DIRECTIONS

In a large bowl, combine the flour, salt, and shortening. It should look like coarse crumbs once the flour, salt, and shortening are combined. Add the egg and incorporate it into the flour mixture. Add water and milk 1 tablespoon at a time.

Mix well until a ball is formed. Wrap the pastry in plastic and refrigerate for 4 hours. This will ensure a flakey crust. Place a saucepan on the stove over medium high heat. Add the bacon and cook until it's done. Add the potato, bay leaf, peas, carrots, celery, shallot, garlic, thyme, wine, broth, lime juice, and salt. Bring it to a boil. Add the shrimp and cook for 3 minutes. In the meantime, in a small bowl, add the water to the flour and mix until a smooth paste is formed.

While the pot is boiling, add the paste while stirring. Once the soup has thickened, turn off the heat. Roll half the pie dough about ¼ of an inch thick onto a clean and lightly floured surface.

(SERVES 4)

PIE CRUST

2 ½ cups of all-purpose flour

1 teaspoon of salt

1 cup of vegetable shortening

1 egg

2 tablespoons of ice cold water

3 tablespoons of ice cold milk

SHRIMP FILLING

2 slices of bacon *(chopped)*

1 small potato *(small dice)*

1 bay leaf

¼ cup of sweet peas

¼ cup diced carrots

¼ cup of diced celery

1 small shallot *(minced)*

2 cloves of garlic *(minced)*

1 teaspoon of thyme

(INGREDIENTS CONTINUE ON NEXT PAGE)

DIRECTIONS (cont.)

Cut the pastry to fit the bottom of the ramekin. Place the ramekin in the oven for 5 minutes until the crust is baked. Remove the ramekins from the oven. Ladle the filling into the ramekins until they are full.

Roll out the remaining pie dough ¼ inch thick. Cut the dough to fit the top of the ramekins. Bake the pies for 15 minutes until the crust is golden brown. Serve immediately.

¼ cup of white wine

1 cup of low sodium chicken broth

1 tablespoon of lime juice

2 teaspoon of salt

½ pound of rock shrimp
  (peeled, deveined, rinsed, drained well)

3 tablespoons of water

3 tablespoons of all-purpose flour

2 six-inch-round custard ramekins

NEW WORLD
RED PESTO SHRIMP

DIRECTIONS

Place the following ingredients into a food processor: tomatoes, sugar, bell pepper, basil, parsley, garlic, and thyme, oregano, and Romano cheese. Cover and blend well (about 20 seconds).

While the food processer is running, remove the mixing lid and pour in the olive oil and butter. Replace the lid and continue to blend the ingredients for an additional 15 seconds. Add the salt and pepper to taste. Set aside.

In a large skillet, sauté the prawns for about 3 minutes, add the above mixture (pesto) to the pan and continue to cook an additional 3 minutes until the prawns are done. Toss with your favorite pasta!

(SERVES 4)

3 Roma tomatoes

½ tablespoon of sugar

1 large bell pepper *(diced)*

2 tablespoons of fresh chopped basil

2 tablespoons of fresh parsley *(chopped)*

4 cloves of crushed garlic

2 teaspoons of dry thyme

2 teaspoons of oregano flakes

¾ cup of grated Romano cheese

¾ cup of extra virgin olive oil

2 tablespoons of melted butter

Salt and pepper to taste

20 jumbo prawns *(peeled and deveined)*

¼ cup of extra virgin olive oil

SOUTHWESTERN
PEPPERED SHRIMP

DIRECTIONS

Preheat a large skillet over medium high heat. Add the sausage and olive oil. Allow the sausage to cook for about 2 minutes. Add the onion, garlic, tomatoes, tomato sauce, sugar and vinegar. Cover the pan and reduce the flame to simmer for about 3 minutes.

In a large bowl, season the shrimp with cumin, turmeric, chili powder, paprika, cayenne pepper, cilantro and black pepper. Add the bell peppers and the prawns to the pan. Cover the pan with a lid and cook for about 4 minutes.

I recommend this dish over linguine or angel hair pasta. Top with Parmesan cheese and savor the flavor.

(SERVES 4)

½ pound of beef smoked sausage

1 tablespoon of extra virgin olive oil

1 small onion *(sliced into strips)*

1 tablespoon of minced garlic

2 small diced tomatoes

1 can of tomato sauce *(15 ounces)*

2 tablespoons of sugar

2 tablespoons of red wine vinegar

1 ½ tablespoons of cumin

½ tablespoon of turmeric

1 tablespoon of chili powder

2 tablespoons of Spanish paprika

2 teaspoons of cayenne pepper

1 tablespoon of cilantro

1 tablespoon of black pepper

20 jumbo prawns *(peeled and deveined)*

½ red bell pepper *(sliced into strips)*

½ green bell pepper *(sliced into strips)*

½ yellow bell pepper *(sliced into strips)*

1 cup of Parmesan cheese

ASIAN
SALMON SAUTÉ

DIRECTIONS

Preheat a large nonstick skillet over medium high heat. Season the salmon with the pepper and garlic. Add the sesame oil to the pan. Place the salmon in the skillet skin side up. Cover the pan with a lid. Sauté the salmon for 3½ minutes, remove the cover and turn the salmon over. Continue to sauté the salmon for an additional 4-5 minutes or until done. Do not overcook the salmon.

Remove the salmon from the pan and arrange on a platter or serving plates. Add to the pan the ginger, soy sauce, vinegar, brown sugar, and scallions. Stir well and simmer the sauce for 1 minute. Spoon the sauce over the salmon and serve.

This dish pairs well with noodles, rice, or grilled vegetables.

(SERVES 4)

4 six-ounce salmon fillets
(bones removed)

1 tablespoon of coarse black pepper

1 tablespoon of garlic powder

2 ½ tablespoons of sesame oil

1 tablespoon of ginger powder

3 tablespoons of low sodium soy sauce

3 tablespoons of rice wine vinegar

1 tablespoon of brown sugar

2 tablespoons of scallions *(chopped)*

BAKED SESAME
SWORDFISH WITH
THAI PURPLE SLAW

DIRECTIONS

In a blender, combine the fish sauce, vinegar, soy sauce, garlic, sesame oil, brown sugar, and pepper flakes. Mix well until the sugar is dissolved (about 15 seconds).

In a medium bowl, combine the cabbage and bell peppers. Pour the sauce into the bowl and toss well. Refrigerate for an hour.

Preheat the oven to 425 degrees. Using a pastry brush, apply the sesame oil to both sides of the swordfish steaks. Season the fish with the garlic powder and sesame seeds. Place the fish on a sheet pan and place it in the oven.

Bake for 12-15 minutes depending on the thickness of the fish. Remove the pan from the oven. Serve the swordfish with the slaw immediately. Enjoy!

(SERVES 4)

SWORDFISH

4 swordfish steaks about 1 inch thick
(rinsed with cold water and patted dry with a paper towel)

¼ cup of sesame oil

1 tablespoon of granulated garlic

1 tablespoon of black sesame seeds

THAI PURPLE SLAW

¼ cup of fish sauce

½ cup of rice wine vinegar

½ cup of low sodium soy sauce

1 tablespoon of minced garlic

2 tablespoons of sesame oil

½ cup of brown sugar

2 teaspoons of crushed red pepper flakes

2 tablespoons of fresh cilantro *(chopped)*

1 small purple cabbage *(shredded)*

1 small red bell pepper *(shredded)*

1 small green bell pepper *(shredded)*

CARIBBEAN TILAPIA
FILLETS

DIRECTIONS

Wash the tilapia fillets and pat them dry with paper towels. In a medium size bowl, combine the flour, salt, and pepper. Place a large skillet on the stove over medium high heat. Pour the olive oil into the pan and warm for about 3 minutes. Coat the fillets with the flour mixture. Immediately place the fillets in the pan. Do not overcrowd the pan. Add a little more oil if necessary.

Sauté the tilapia fillets for 3 minutes on each side. Repeat this step until all the fillets are cooked. Place the tilapia on a serving platter or plates and keep warm until ready to serve.

Add the onion, garlic, pepper flakes, cumin seeds and ginger to the pan and sauté for 3 minutes. Stir in the brown sugar until dissolved. Add the soy sauce, maple syrup, vinegar, and lemon juice. Simmer the sauce until it thickens (about 5 minutes).

Spoon the sauce over the fish. Garnish with the scallions. Serve immediately!

(SERVES 4-6)

4-6 tilapia fillets

1 cup of all-purpose flour

1 tablespoon of salt

1 tablespoon of ground black pepper

½ cup of extra virgin olive oil

½ Vidalia onion *(chopped)*

1 tablespoon of minced garlic

1 teaspoon of crushed red pepper flakes

1 teaspoon of cumin seed

2 teaspoons of ground ginger

2 tablespoons of light brown sugar

½ cup of light soy sauce *(low sodium)*

1 tablespoon of maple syrup

½ cup of cider vinegar

1 tablespoon of lemon juice

3 tablespoons of chopped scallions

GRILLED MAHI-MAHI
WITH FRESH FRUIT SALSA

DIRECTIONS

Place the salsa ingredients in a medium-size bowl. Mix well and refrigerate for about an hour prior to use. This will allow all the flavors proper time to blend well.

Preheat the grill for about 20 minutes before use.

In a mixing bowl, combine the ingredients for the marinade and mix well. Use a pastry brush to apply the marinade to the Mahi fillets. Place the fish on the grill. Grill the fish for about 3½ minutes on each side. Remove the fillets from the grill and place them on a platter. Spoon the salsa over the fish just before serving.

(SERVES 4)

MARINADE

2 tablespoons of extra virgin olive oil

Juice of 3 limes

½ tablespoon of sea salt

½ tablespoon of cracked black pepper

1 tablespoon of minced garlic

2 teaspoons of Dijon mustard

4 Mahi-Mahi fillets
(washed and patted dry with a paper towel)

SALSA

3 tablespoons of diced pineapple chunks

3 tablespoons of diced mango

3 tablespoons of diced papaya

1 diced Granny Smith apple

1 small diced Vidalia onion

1 tablespoon of minced cilantro

Juice of 1 lime

1 small jalapeño *(chopped)*

GRILLED RED SNAPPER WITH GINGER LEMONGRASS SAUCE

DIRECTIONS

Preheat the grill to medium high heat. In a large sealable container, combine all the ingredients for the marinade and mix well. Place each fillet in the container. Refrigerate for 30 minutes to an hour. Remove the fish from the refrigerator and place on the grill. Cook the fish skin side down for about 6 minutes. In the meantime, place the ingredients for the sauce in a blender. Blend for about 15 to 20 seconds. Once the fish is cooked, transfer the fish from the grill to a platter. Spoon the sauce over the fish. Use any remaining sauce over your favorite vegetables or rice. Garnish the fish with lime slices and cilantro. Enjoy!

(SERVES 4)

4 large red snapper fillets
(cleaned and patted dry with a paper towel)

MARINADE

1 ½ tablespoons of ground coriander

2 tablespoons of minced garlic

2 teaspoons of cayenne pepper

1 tablespoon of sea salt

1 tablespoon of dried thyme

1 tablespoon of chopped fresh parsley

1 tablespoon of chopped fresh cilantro

1 tablespoon of white pepper

¾ cup of lime juice

½ cup of extra virgin olive oil

SAUCE

½ cup of Thai fish sauce

½ tablespoon of ground ginger

3 minced lemongrass bulbs
(white base only, trimmed outer leaves peeled off)

½ cup of rice wine vinegar

½ cup of lime juice

½ cup of sugar

BROILED
SEA BASS WITH
CRANBERRY CASHEW SAUCE

DIRECTIONS

Heat a large ovenproof skillet on the stove on medium high heat. Place the olive oil and 2 tablespoons of butter in the pan. Season the bass with salt, garlic, pepper, paprika and parsley. Place the bass in the pan skin side up; sauté the bass for 3 minutes. Turn the bass over and place the pan in the oven for 8-10 minutes to finish cooking.

Remove the skillet from the oven and place on the stove on medium high heat. Place the bass on a platter and cover to remain warm. Remove any skin left over from the fish and discard. Add to the skillet the butter, garlic, shallot, cranberries, cashews, soy sauce, lime juice and chicken broth. Allow the sauce to simmer for about 2 minutes. Spoon the sauce over the fish and serve immediately.

(SERVES 6)

¼ cup of extra virgin olive oil

2 tablespoons of unsalted butter

6 large sea bass portions

1½ tablespoons of sea salt

1 tablespoon of garlic powder

1 tablespoon of cracked black pepper

2 teaspoons of paprika

1 tablespoon of fresh chopped parsley

SAUCE

1 cup of unsalted butter *(melted)*

2 tablespoons of minced garlic

1 small shallot *(minced)*

3 tablespoons of dried cranberries

3 tablespoons cashew halves

¼ cup of light soy sauce

2 tablespoons of lime juice

¼ cup of chicken broth

PREHEAT the oven to 475 degrees.

BLACKENED
PERCH FILLETS

DIRECTIONS

Wash the fillets and pat them dry with a paper towel. Set aside. Melt the salted butter and set aside. Preheat the skillet over high heat. In a bowl, combine all the dry ingredients and mix well. Coat each fillet with the melted butter. Place each fillet into the seasoning mix.

Coat the fillets well. Immediately place the fillets into the skillet. Do not overcrowd the pan. Cook each fillet for about 2-3 minutes on each side. Some fillets may take a little longer to cook depending on the thickness of each one.

When the fillets are flakey, that indicates they are done. Remove the fillets from the skillet and place on a platter. Squeeze a lemon wedge over the fish for added flavor. Garnish with the remaining lemon wedges and fresh cilantro. Enjoy!

(SERVES 4-6)

7 or 8 ocean perch fillets
 (about 8 ounces each)

½ cup of melted butter *(salted)*

BLACKENED SEASONING

THIS SEASONING CAN BE PREPARED AHEAD OF TIME.

1 tablespoon of seasoned salt

2 tablespoons of paprika

3 teaspoons of cayenne pepper

1 tablespoon of garlic powder

1 tablespoon of onion powder

3 teaspoons of black pepper

3 teaspoons of dried thyme

3 teaspoons of oregano flakes

2 teaspoons of tarragon

8 lemon wedges

1 bunch of fresh cilantro

NOTE: YOU WILL NEED TWO VERY IMPORTANT THINGS—PLENTY OF VENTILATION AND A LARGE CAST IRON SKILLET.

BROILED
TROUT WITH
LEMON CREAM SAUCE

DIRECTIONS

Preheat the oven to broil. Using a cast iron skillet or an oven- proof pan, coat the bottom of the pan with nonstick spray. Season the trout with olive oil, sea salt, lemon juice, garlic, tarragon, thyme, and black pepper. Place the pan in the oven and broil for 4½-5 minutes. Remove the fish from the oven when finished and set aside.

Place a saucepan on the stove over medium high heat. Add the cream, lemon juice, paprika, Tabasco sauce, salt and ground pepper. Mix well. Lower the heat to a simmer. Cook for about 3 minutes to reduce sauce while stirring constantly. Use a ladle to apply the sauce over the trout. Garnish with fresh dill. Serve immediately.

(SERVES 4)

TROUT

4 large rainbow trout fillets
(washed and patted dry with a paper towel)

3 tablespoons of olive oil

Sea salt to taste

Juice of 3 lemons

Garlic powder to taste

1 tablespoon of tarragon leaves *(chopped)*

1 teaspoon of thyme

4 teaspoons of ground black pepper

LEMON CREAM SAUCE

1 ½ cups of heavy cream

Juice of 1 lemon

1 teaspoon of paprika

1 tablespoon of Tabasco sauce

1 pinch of salt

1 teaspoon of ground pepper

4 fresh sprigs of dill

ROAST TURKEY & WATERCRESS HOAGIE

DIRECTIONS

Place the tenderloin in a casserole dish. Rub the oil liberally onto the tenderloin. Season the tenderloin with the poultry seasoning, thyme, oregano, garlic, pepper, paprika, and rotisserie seasoning. Bake for 12-17 minutes or until done; remove the turkey from the oven and cool for about 10 minutes.

Split the bread in half lengthwise. Set aside. In a bowl, combine the cranberry sauce, horseradish, cilantro, and feta cheese. Spread the mixture on the bottom half of the bread. Arrange the watercress onto the bottom half of the loaf. Slice the turkey on an angle and layer the slices onto the hoagie. Mix the sour cream and garlic together and apply to the top half of the bread.

(SERVINGS WILL VARY)

1 turkey tenderloin *(8-12 ounce)*

¼ cup of olive oil

2 teaspoons of poultry seasoning

1 tablespoon of chopped thyme

1 tablespoon of chopped oregano

1 tablespoon of minced garlic powder

2 teaspoons of black pepper

2 teaspoons of paprika

1 teaspoon of rotisserie seasoning

1 French baguette

¼ cup of cranberry sauce

1 tablespoon of horseradish

1 tablespoon of chopped cilantro

2 tablespoons of crumbled feta cheese

1½ cups of watercress
(rinsed and dried well)

½ cup of sour cream

½ tablespoon of minced garlic

PREHEAT the oven to 400 degrees.

BROILED PORK TENDERLOIN
WITH CHERRY COGNAC GLAZE

DIRECTIONS

In a medium size bowl, add the flour, salt, garlic, and pepper. Mix well. Coat the tenderloins with the flour mixture. Place an ovenproof skillet on the stove over medium high heat. Add the olive oil to the pan and heat the oil (about 2 minutes). Sauté the pork in the olive oil until browned on all sides. Remove the pan from the heat and place in the oven for 12 minutes or until desired internal temperature is reached. (Use a meat thermometer for testing.)

Remove the tenderloins from the oven and return the pan to the stove. Place the tenderloins onto a cutting board to rest. Meanwhile, add the cherries to the pan and stir until thawed and heated through. Once the cherries are heated through, remove the pan from the stove and pour the cognac into the pan. Return the pan to the stove and allow the alcohol to burn off. Reduce the heat to simmer for about 3-4 minutes (the alcohol may ignite, so be careful and don't panic).

Slice the tenderloins about 1¼ inch thick. Pour half the sauce onto the plate or platter. Arrange the pork on a plate or platter, and then pour the remaining sauce over the pork. Garnish with fresh rosemary. Enjoy!

(SERVES 4)

2 fresh pork tenderloins
(washed, with silver skin and excess fat removed)

1 cup of all-purpose flour

½ tablespoon of salt

1 tablespoon of granulated garlic

½ tablespoon of coarse black pepper

¼ cup of extra virgin olive oil

½ cup of frozen cherries

1 ounce of cognac

Fresh rosemary for garnish

PREHEAT the oven to 400 degrees.

PEPPERCORN PORK TENDERLOIN
WITH FOREST OF MUSHROOMS

DIRECTIONS

In a small bowl, combine the flour, salt and granulated garlic. Mix well. Place a large oven- proof skillet on the stove over medium high heat. Add only 2 of the tablespoons of the butter and all of the olive oil. Coat the tenderloins in the flour mixture, shake off the excess flour and place immediately into the skillet. Brown the tenderloins on all sides. Place in the preheated oven for about 12 minutes.

Remove the skillet from the oven and return to the stove over medium high heat. Remove the tenderloins from the skillet and place on a cutting board. Allow the tenderloins to sit for about 2 minutes. Slice and arrange on a platter or plate. Add to the skillet the peppercorns, mushrooms, thyme, and basil.

Sauté the mushrooms for about 1 minute, add the sherry (the alcohol may ignite, so be careful and don't panic) and allow it to reduce for an additional minute. Stir in the remaining butter until melted and then pour over the tenderloins.

Serve immediately.

(SERVES 4)

2 fresh pork tenderloins
   (washed, fat and silver skin removed)

1 cup of all-purpose flour

1 tablespoon of seasoned salt

1 tablespoon of granulated garlic

3 tablespoons of unsalted butter

2 tablespoons of extra virgin olive oil

1 tablespoon of 3-peppercorn mix
   (cracked black pepper, green peppercorn, and pink peppercorn)

½ cup each of baby Bella, shiitake, button, crimini mushrooms

2 teaspoons of dry thyme

2 teaspoons of dry basil

⅓ cup of sherry wine

PERUVIAN PORK
MEDALLIONS WITH
SPINACH PESTO SAUCE

DIRECTIONS

Warm a large skillet over medium high heat. Combine the flour, black pepper, and seasoned salt. Mix well. Add the olive oil to the skillet. Slice the tenderloin into 1-inch pieces.

Toss the tenderloin medallions in the flour mixture. Shake off the excess flour and then immediately place the tenderloin medallions in the skillet. Sauté the tenderloins for about 2 minutes on each side, and leave them in the skillet; remove the skillet from heat.

In a small skillet, sauté the onion, garlic, and pine nuts in the olive oil until the onions are translucent (about two minutes). Place the spinach in a blender along with the onions, garlic, pine nuts, basil, milk, and cheese. Process the mixture until it's smooth. Add the salt and pepper to taste.

Adjust the flavors if necessary with additional salt and pepper. Add a little more milk if too thick. Pour the sauce over the pork and simmer for up to 2 minutes. Serve immediately.

(SERVES 2)

PORK

1 pork tenderloin
(washed, fat and silver skin removed)

3 tablespoons of all-purpose flour

2 teaspoons of coarse black pepper

1 teaspoon of seasoned salt

2 tablespoons of extra virgin olive oil

SPINACH PESTO

1 onion *(chopped)*

3 cloves of garlic

¼ cup of pine nuts

2 tablespoons of extra virgin olive oil

3 ½ cups of baby spinach

½ cup of fresh basil

¾ cup of milk

½ cup of shredded pepper jack cheese

Salt and pepper to taste

ADOBO
PORK CHOPS WITH
BLACK BEANS AND RICE

DIRECTIONS

Using a blender, combine cider vinegar, soy sauce, orange juice, garlic, seasoned salt, cumin, oregano, black pepper, coriander, cinnamon, mustard, crushed red pepper flakes, shallot and brown sugar.

Blend well for about 1 minute. Place the pork chops and marinade in a sealable container (Ziploc or plastic container with a good-fitting lid).

Chill from 6-24 hours. Combine the black bean mixture and chill for about 30 minutes prior to use. Preheat the oven to 400 degrees.

Place the chops and marinade in an ovenproof pan or skillet. Cover for the first 15 minutes. Bake uncovered for the last 5 minutes. Cook the rice in chicken broth instead of water. Remove the chops from the oven.

(SERVES 4)

PORK

4 pork loin chops
(washed and patted dry)

½ cup of cider vinegar

¼ cup of low sodium soy sauce

¼ cup of orange juice

4 cloves of garlic

1 teaspoon of seasoned salt

1 teaspoon of cumin

1 teaspoon of dry oregano

1 teaspoon of cracked black pepper

1 teaspoon of coriander

1 teaspoon of cinnamon

1 teaspoon of dry mustard

1 teaspoon of crushed red pepper flakes

1 shallot *(diced)*

2 tablespoons of brown sugar

(INGREDIENTS CONTINUE ON NEXT PAGE)

DIRECTIONS (cont.)

Plate the rice and chops. Spoon the black beans over the chops. Spoon the marinade over the rice and chops. Enjoy!

RICE

IN A SMALL POT, COMBINE AND COOK:

2 ½ cups of chicken broth

1 ½ cups of brown rice

BEANS

IN A SMALL BOWL, COMBINE:

1 small can of black beans
(rinsed and drained)

1 small red onion (chopped)

1 teaspoon of ground cumin

1 tablespoon of cilantro (chopped)

1 medium tomato (diced)

2 tablespoons of lime juice

2 tablespoons of olive oil

HERB-CRUSTED
LEG OF LAMB

DIRECTIONS

Add the mustard liberally to the lamb. Apply the spices and herbs evenly over the entire lamb. Place the lamb on a roaster rack and set aside for a moment.

Pour the diced tomatoes and sugar along with the vegetable and beef broth into the bottom of the roaster and mix well. Place the lamb and the rack in the roaster. Cover with foil or a lid. Cook the lamb for 2 ½ hours. Remove the roaster from the oven.

Lift the lamb out of the roaster and place onto a platter. Pour the sauce into a small saucepot and bring to a boil. Add the water to the cornstarch and blend until a smooth paste is formed.

Using a wire whip, add the paste to the boiling sauce. Once the sauce begins to thicken, reduce the heat to simmer while continuing to stir. Spoon the sauce over the lamb and enjoy!

(SERVINGS WILL VARY)

1 large leg of lamb
  (rinsed, then patted dry)

2 tablespoons of Dijon mustard

2 tablespoons of kosher salt

1 tablespoon of cracked black pepper

2 tablespoons of fresh rosemary *(chopped)*

2 tablespoons of fresh basil *(chopped)*

1 tablespoon of thyme

1 tablespoon of sage *(chopped)*

1 teaspoon of ground cumin

2 teaspoons of paprika

2 15- ounce cans of stewed tomatoes

1 tablespoon of sugar

3 cups of vegetable broth

1 cup of beef broth

¼ cup of cornstarch

¼ cup of water

PREHEAT the oven to 350 degrees.

STUFFED
CHICKEN ROULADE

DIRECTIONS

Spread plastic wrap over a cutting board (about 12 inches wide). Place the chicken breasts onto the plastic 2 at a time. Cover the chicken with an additional sheet of plastic. Pound the chicken breasts until nice and thin. This will make the chicken pliable and easy to fold. Repeat the steps for the final 2 chicken breasts.

Using a pastry brush, spread the melted butter over each piece of chicken. Place 2 pieces of Brie into each breast. Add the tomatoes, spinach, and garlic. Roll and tuck the breasts at both ends.

Secure with a toothpick or butcher's twine. In a small bowl, combine the eggs and milk (mix well). Set aside. In a small bowl, combine the flour, garlic, pepper, and salt. Set aside. In a small bowl add the bread crumbs and set aside. Roll the breasts into the flour mixture. Shake off the excess flour. Place the breasts into the egg and milk mixture.

Immediately roll the breasts into the bread crumbs. In a large ovenproof skillet, place

(SERVES 4)

4 six-ounce boneless skinless chicken breasts
(butterflied and thinly pounded)

½ cup of salted butter *(melted)*

8 slices of Brie cheese

¾ cup of sundried tomatoes in oil

3 cups of frozen spinach
(thawed and drained well)

2 tablespoons of minced garlic

3 large eggs *(beaten)*

¼ cup of milk

1 cup of all-purpose flour

2 teaspoons of garlic powder

2 teaspoons of black pepper

1 teaspoon of salt

3 cups of Japanese bread crumbs

1 ½ cups extra virgin olive oil

PREHEAT the oven to 400 degrees.

DIRECTIONS (cont.)

the olive oil in the pan and heat on medium high. Place the breasts in the pan and lightly brown on all sides. Place the entire pan in the oven and continue baking the breasts for about 10-12 minutes. Do not overcook. Remove the skillet from the oven. Arrange the breasts on a platter; garnish and serve.

GRILLED QUAIL

DIRECTIONS

Quail is a very delicate bird and cooks in a short period of time. Do not overcook the quail.

In a medium bowl, combine the garlic, cumin, thyme, cilantro, chili powder, pepper and salt. Mix well. Add the lime juice and stir. While stirring the mixture, add the olive oil and continue stirring for about 30 seconds. Place the quail in the bowl or a large sealable plastic bag.

Pour the liquid over the quail and refrigerate 2 to 4 fours. Remove the quail from the refrigerator. Prepare your grill over medium high heat. Place the quail on the grill and cook for 3 minutes on each side. Remove the quail from the grill and arrange on a serving platter. Garnish with fresh lime slices and cilantro.

(SERVES 4)

4 split quails
(washed and patted dry)

1 tablespoon of minced garlic

2 teaspoons of cumin

2 teaspoons of dried thyme

1 tablespoon of chopped cilantro

1 tablespoon of chili powder

2 teaspoons of coarse black pepper

Pinch of salt

1 cup of lime juice

1/2 cup of extra virgin olive oil

2 slices of lime *(garnish)*

Fresh cilantro *(garnish)*

STUFFED CHICKEN
&SHRIMP

DIRECTIONS

Place the chicken breasts on a nonstick flat baking sheet. Divide the Boursin cheese into 4 parts. Spread a portion over each breast. In the following order place the pepper jack cheese, spinach, shrimp, carrots and sliced butter over each breast.

Carefully roll the breasts and tuck each end of the chicken until fully closed. Secure each breast with a toothpick or butcher's twine.

In a large frying pan, preheat the olive oil on medium high. In a large bowl, combine the pepper, salt, and garlic powder. Mix well. Coat each chicken breast in the flour mixture. Shake off the excess flour.

Immediately place the breast in the oil. Brown the breast on all sides for about 2-3 minutes. Drain well. Place the breasts on a baking sheet and place them in the oven for 12 minutes or until done. Remove the breasts from the oven and cool for about 2 minutes. Slice the breasts and serve with your favorite sides.

(SERVES 4)

4 large chicken breasts
(washed and butterflied, patted dry)

12 ounces of Boursin cheese

4 slices of pepper jack cheese

½ pound of frozen spinach
(thawed, chopped, and drained well)

½ pound of large shrimp
(washed, peeled, deveined, chopped)

4 tablespoons of matchstick carrots

½ pound of large shrimp
(washed, peeled, deveined, chopped)

4 tablespoons of salted butter
(chilled and sliced)

3 cups of extra virgin olive oil

1 cup of flour

2 teaspoons of black pepper

2 teaspoons of salt

2 teaspoons of garlic powder

PREHEAT the oven to 425 degrees.

FAMILY, **FRIENDS &** MY MOST REQUESTED DISHES

IN THE FIRST SECTION of this book, The Early Years, I mentioned the assortment of good cooks in my family and the fact that I'm not the only chef. In particular, I referenced my father, along with various aunts and uncles and grandparents who have all made an impression on my cooking. As I open this chapter, I reminisce about certain meals that really stuck with me. My Uncle Jimmy has had a tremendous effect on the way I approach food.

Our family's very first chef, Uncle Gene, was the man. As a little boy, I can remember tasting his chicken mozzarella for the first time. The tomato sauce was so rich and the cheese was so stringy that it never seemed to break. That was one dish that I will never forget. Uncle Gene doesn't cook as much these days. Of course he's much older now. He lived most of his life in Delaware, but now resides in North Carolina with my cousin Russell.

Our family's ***very first chef,*** UNCLE GENE, WAS THE MAN.

Every now and then I can go by Russell's house and catch Uncle Gene cooking something that still smells like he's at the top of his game. We've often talked about how he got his start and some of his favorite dishes. His son Travis now carries the torch and is a great chef in his own right. It's a beautiful thing when we all get together and talk about food. My cousin Ed and I share cooking tips and recipes all the time. I look forward to passing along these tips to the next generation of cooks in the family.

I love it when I host an event and everyone is graciously raving over my cooking. After all, my goal is to satisfy my clients and their guests. Not surprisingly, many people enjoy trying new things and are often delighted to go outside of their comfort zone. I can remember the first time that I made Lobster Pancakes. I received various responses from people. Some immediately said, "Wow, I can't wait to try that", while others were a lot more hesitant. The sweetness of the pancake and the earthiness of the fresh herbs tossed into the mix make a great combination that can really dance on the palate.

So the next obvious question has been, "Do you put syrup on it?" The answer is no. For some reason, I've come to really enjoy the taste of apricot. I start with a stick of butter in the pan. I add in a jar of apricot jam. I mix it until the jam has melted and has blended with the butter.

I add a tablespoon of brown sugar, a tablespoon of Dijon mustard, two tablespoons of low sodium soy sauce, a pinch of crushed red pepper, a tablespoon of chopped scallions, and finish it off with sesame oil.

It seems like every time I come to Rocky Mount, someone is waiting for me to make the cabbage. I guess If that's the dish that's going to make people happy, then I'm all for it. When I was working for Byron Cage, I quickly learned that he's a fan of Brussels sprouts. Not too many people I know are fans of Brussels sprouts, so I had to come up with a special presentation. I wanted to give him something other than the typical bacon and onion sauté or just blanching them in some kind of broth. That's why I love the Italian Brussels sprouts recipe. It's become a fan of many. My cabbage recipes have

The *funny* thing is
I CAME UP **WITH THIS DISH** ONE DAY
WHILE *TAKING A SHOWER.*

Who would have thought to put those items together? This is my most requested dish to date. The funny thing is I came up with this dish one day while taking a shower.

I seem to come up with my dishes at the strangest times. It's not from looking at a host of television shows, as some might guess. To the contrary, most of my dishes are inspired by the time I spend with family. When I travel, ideas often jump out at me at the oddest of times or places. I consider the time I passed a cabbage patch in Tarboro, North Carolina, to be one of them. I love cabbage, but not as much as my sister Tricia.

become some of the most popular dishes that I prepare.

One of the things that come with the territory of being a chef is that everywhere I go it seems I'm always presented with a question about a recipe gone wrong. It's just one of those things I can expect. It doesn't bother me, but I often wonder how long before the next time I'm presented with a "how-to" recipe question. I guess it keeps me on my toes. That should cause any chef to continue to study.

Another one of my most requested dishes is the Champagne Chicken recipe. While

I was working for Benvenue Country club in Rocky Mount, North Carolina, Chef Larry Kennedy introduced this dish to me. It instantly became my favorite chicken dish. It's simple to make and very tasty. It incorporates a cream-based sauce that can be served at a banquet or during a regular Sunday meal. Most people want to know what kind of champagne is in the dish, but the answer to that is there is "a very good one". I do use a very good chardonnay for the recipe as well. Champagne or sparkling wine can be substituted for the chardonnay without incident.

One of my favorite meals is oxtails. I love beef. There's been a lot of discussion about red meat and how often it should be consumed or how it should be prepared. It's simple; red meat stays in your system for three days. We should eat lean cuts of beef if we're going to consume it at all. I say buy good cuts, say grace, and enjoy. When I prepare oxtails, I usually trim the majority of the fat off before I cook them. Most people are still wondering where oxtails come from. They come from the tail of a cow. In the old days, oxtails would come from oxen. But times have changed. If you like beef, you'll love oxtails. I like them with rice or mashed potatoes.

I love to entertain family and friends. For me, my idea of a good time consists of having family, fried fish, and a good "spades" game. I remember days of sitting up with family and friends all night while doing just that. There's nothing like family and I have come to learn that true friends are few and far between. We should cherish them both.

My mother now suffers from Alzheimer's disease. It's amazing that she spent well over 20 years of her life dedicated to cooking for the community and feeding those who were unable to feed themselves. Oftentimes my sisters Amanda and Tricia and I would sit around with other family members and reminisce about some of the terrific meals that she would put together. One such meal is her salmon croquettes recipe, which I've included in this book. She always had a way of creating something out of nothing.

There were many days I would come into the kitchen thinking we weren't going to have much on the table, but my mother knew how to put it together. I can remember my mother literally bringing people in off the street and feeding them from our table. At first, I didn't understand why. The whole time I would be thinking "How can we afford to give food away? Especially to people we didn't even know!" It was almost as if she knew who was in need and purposefully sought them out. Looking back on it, I can see why she was so blessed. It's one of those simple principles of life. Give and you will receive. We never missed a meal and we always had enough.

We lived in Ohio for a few years. I'll never forget the garden my mother and my uncle Larry planted. We had peppers, squash, greens, and tomatoes. Everything was so fresh. The taste of everything we grew was so much better than what we had purchased from any store. As I think about it, that should have been the way everything tasted. My mother grew up on farms. My grandparents were sharecroppers in North Carolina.

My grandfather grew everything from tobacco, corn, peanuts, collard greens, tomatoes, pigs and chickens. You name it, they grew it. So, my mother knew exactly what she was doing with that simple garden. She knew how to survive and how to multiply her bounty. She never wasted anything. Believe it or not, as chefs, we also learn not to waste anything. Some of my best soups or sauces come from items that most people would throw away. A great example of that comes from onions. Did you know that the peel of an onion has more flavors in it than the actual onion? Once I learned that, I used unpeeled onions for every stockpot.

Every now and then, I like to have something simple to snack on. Chips and dip always go together. I remember doing an interview on the "700 Club." My son and daughter were on the show with me. We were talking about simple, healthy snacks that kids would like

to eat. We had fresh fruit on skewers and a black bean and corn salsa. One of the amusing things about kids is they will say the funniest things. You never see it coming. As we were preparing the salsa, I made the comment that my children loved that particular salsa. Subsequently, my son was asked whether he liked it. He said, "Not really." I wanted to go to commercial so bad. It was hard to keep a straight face after that. My son threw me under the bus on national television!

The crazy part about the whole scenario is, right after the show, the producer pointed out that my son was eating the salsa as if he were starving. He even had the nerve to ask whether we could take the rest of it with us. That was too funny. That's one snack I will never forget. Thank you Joshua and Jasmine for simply being you. I love you!

I dedicate this chapter to my family, friends, and those of you who have shared your favorite dishes during the course of this flavorful journey. It is my hope that you all will continue to enjoy the effort that goes into every dish. Let's eat!

Thank you **Joshua and Jasmine**
FOR SIMPLY BEING YOU.

LOBSTER
PANCAKES

DIRECTIONS

Place a large skillet on the stove over medium heat. Pour the butter into the pan. Add the lobster to the pan. Add the garlic, scallions, and bell pepper to the pan and sauté for about 4-5 minutes.

Remove the lobster from the pan and place in a small bowl for later use. In a large bowl, combine the flour, sugar, baking powder, and salt. Mix well. In a separate bowl, combine the buttermilk, milk, and eggs. Mix well. Pour the milk and egg mixture into the flour and mix well. Allow the batter to sit for about 5 minutes.

Place a large skillet on the stove over medium high heat. Place 2 tablespoons of butter in the pan. Fill a 1/3 measure cup with the batter. Pour the batter into the pan and repeat until the pan is filled with pancakes.

(SERVES 4-6)

¼ cup of unsalted butter *(melted)*

4 ounces of fresh lobster meat *(diced)*

2 teaspoons of garlic *(minced)*

2 tablespoons of scallions *(chopped)*

1 tablespoon of red bell pepper *(minced)*

3 cups of all-purpose flour

3 tablespoons of white sugar

3 teaspoons of baking powder

Pinch of salt

3 cups of buttermilk

½ cup of milk

3 eggs

⅓ cup of unsalted butter *(melted)*

Do not crowd the pan. Portion the lobster mix into the pancakes. Allow the pancakes to cook for about 30 seconds on each side or until the edges become golden. Turn only once.

Remove the pancakes and place on a platter. Repeat the steps until the batter is gone. My **Apricot Dipping Sauce** (page 32) gives a great twist instead of the usual syrup we traditionally have with our pancakes.

CRAB-STUFFED SHRIMP
AND CRAB CAKES

DIRECTIONS

Wash the shrimp well and ensure all the veins are removed. Drain well and set aside. Open the crab and drain most of the liquid but not all. Pour the crab into a large bowl. Check the crab to make sure the shells have been removed.

Place a large skillet on the stove and preheat over medium. Pour 1 tablespoon of butter in the pan and sauté the bell pepper, garlic, and shallot for about 4 minutes or until the vegetables are soft. Pour the mixture into the crab. To the bowl add the mustard, Worcestershire, lemon juice, bay seasoning, and sugar, egg, and bread crumbs. Gently mix the crab but do not over mix. Divide the crab in half. Use a tablespoon to measure the crab for the stuffed shrimp. Form a ball of each crab mixture and place onto the shrimp. Fold the tail of the shrimp over the crab to secure. Use a nonstick cookie sheet. Set the shrimp on the cookie sheet. Place the pan in the preheated oven and bake for 12 minutes or until done.

(SERVES 4)

12 large shrimp
(size 16-20, peeled, deveined, tail on, and butterflied)

1 pound of jumbo lump crab meat

3 tablespoons of unsalted butter *(melted)*
(reserve 2 tablespoons for later use)

1 tablespoon of minced red bell pepper

1 tablespoon of minced garlic

1 tablespoon of minced shallot

½ tablespoon of Dijon mustard

½ tablespoon of Worcestershire sauce

Juice of ½ lemon

2 teaspoons of bay seasoning

2 teaspoons of sugar

1 egg *(beaten)*

2 tablespoons of plain bread crumbs

PREHEAT the oven to 425 degrees.

SHRIMP & SCALLOP
PEPPERED SALAD
WITH **CITRUS VINAIGRETTE**

DIRECTIONS

Place a large skillet onto the stove and warm over medium high. Season the prawns and scallops with paprika, black pepper, garlic, zest and lemon juice; sauté for about 2 minutes. Add the celery, onion, and dill. Continue to cook for 4 minutes more. Remove the prawns and scallops from the stove. Set aside. Divide the greens onto two plates. Arrange the prawns and scallops evenly over the greens.

In a large bowl, combine the shallot, vinegar, orange juice, mustard, honey, and salt. Mix well. While mixing, add the olive oil until well blended. Pour the vinaigrette over the salad evenly and enjoy.

(SERVES 2)

12 large prawns

8 colossal sea scallops

½ tablespoon of bay seasoning

½ tablespoon of paprika

½ tablespoon of coarse black pepper

½ tablespoon of minced garlic

Zest of 1 lemon

½ cup of lemon juice

½ cup of extra virgin olive oil

1 cup of minced celery

1 cup of chopped red onion

2 tablespoons of chopped dill

2 cups of mixed field greens
(washed and drained well)

CITRUS VINAIGRETTE

½ shallot *(minced)*

2 tablespoons of champagne vinegar

½ cup of fresh squeezed orange juice

3 teaspoons of Dijon mustard

1 tablespoon of honey

2 pinches of salt

2 tablespoons of extra virgin olive oil

ITALIAN ROASTED VEAL CHOPS WITH HERBED TOMATO SAUCE

DIRECTIONS

Rinse the veal chops in cold water. Drain well and pat dry with a paper towel. Coat the chops with Dijon mustard. In a large bowl, combine the fresh herbs, pepper, garlic, and seasoned salt with the Italian bread crumbs. Mix well.

Place a large skillet on the stove over medium high heat. Pour the olive oil into the skillet. Coat the chops with the bread mixture. Immediately place the chops in the skillet 2 at a time. Brown the chops for about 30 seconds on each side. Place the chops on a sheet pan with a rack if possible. Place in the oven and bake for 12–15 minutes or until desired cooking temperature is reached.

In the meantime, place a saucepot on the stove on medium high heat. Add the olive oil to the pan. Once the oil is hot, add the tomatoes to the pot. Sauté for about 2 minutes, add the remaining ingredients and stir well. Cover and turn the heat down to simmer for 10 minutes.

(SERVES 4)

4 bone-in veal loin chops
(Frenched or the bone cleaned)

3 tablespoons of Dijon mustard

2 tablespoons of fresh rosemary *(chopped)*

2 tablespoons of fresh thyme *(chopped)*

2 tablespoons of fresh basil *(chopped)*

1 tablespoon of coarse black pepper

1 tablespoon of garlic powder

1 tablespoon of seasoned salt

3 cups of Italian bread crumbs

1 cup of extra virgin olive oil

RESERVE 1½ TABLESPOONS OF THE CHOPPED HERBS

HERBED TOMATO SAUCE

1 tablespoon of extra virgin olive oil

4 Roma tomatoes *(diced)*

½ cup of beef broth

½ cup of chicken broth

2 tablespoons of sugar

(INGREDIENTS CONTINUE ON NEXT PAGE)

DIRECTIONS (cont.)

Remove the chops from the oven. Ladle the sauce onto the serving plate. Arrange the chops onto the sauce and serve.

1 ½ tablespoons of chopped herbs
(reserved from above)

½ cup of dry red wine

¼ cup of balsamic vinegar

4 ounces of tomato paste

AL'S
ULTIMATE FILET

ONE OF THE THINGS I really enjoy about being a chef is that I get to meet a lot of great people. Every so often I will have the blessing of making a new friend. I was hired by a wonderful couple to do some cooking over a two-week period. Yes! It was Lavern and Al. I can remember showing up each morning and seeing Lavern with that beautiful smile, waiting to hear what was on the menu for that day.

But then, there was my main man Al. His friends call him Big Al. Al told me the favorite thing that I prepared for him was the filet. There's nothing like the smell of a coffee-rubbed steak, which is what I used for Al's filet. It's very southwestern bbq in its approach, so here's to you Al. I call this Al's Ultimate Filet.

DIRECTIONS

Place a cast iron skillet on the stove on high heat. Coat the filets on each side with the olive oil. In a small bowl, combine the chili powder, paprika, cumin, coriander, garlic,

(SERVES 2)

2 filets mignon *(10-ounce)*

2 tablespoons of olive oil

¼ cup of ground coffee

¼ cup of Ancho chili powder

1 tablespoon of Spanish paprika

1 tablespoon of cumin

1 tablespoon of coriander

1 tablespoon of garlic powder

1 tablespoon of dry mustard

1 tablespoon of seasoned salt

½ tablespoon of thyme

½ tablespoon of coarse black pepper

2 tablespoons of butter

1 tablespoon of fresh parsley *(chopped)*

1 onion *(sliced)*

4 baby Bella mushrooms

PREHEAT the oven to 450 degrees.

DIRECTIONS (cont.)

mustard, salt, thyme and black pepper. Liberally coat the filets in the rub.

Place the filets in the hot skillet and sear for about 3 minutes on each side. Place the skillet in the oven and continue to cook for 12 minutes. Remove the skillet from the oven and return to the stove.

Place the filets on a cutting board or plate. Allow the filets to rest for about 5 minutes before slicing. Place the butter, parsley, onion, and mushrooms in the skillet.

Sauté for about 4 minutes. To serve, spoon the onion-mushroom topping over the filets. I hope you all enjoy this as much as Al did.

LOLLIPOP
LAMB CHOPS

DIRECTIONS

Place a large skillet on the stove over medium high heat. Add the olive oil and butter to the skillet and reduce the heat to low. Rub the lamb with mustard liberally on all sides.

Season the lamb with the salt and pepper on all sides. Return the heat to medium high. Slice the lamb between each rib. Place each chop into the pan. Sauté the lamb chops for 3 minutes.

Add the garlic, rosemary, thyme, Worcestershire sauce, and soy sauce. Turn the lamb chops over and continue to simmer for 3 additional minutes or until desired temperature is reached. Spoon the sauce over potatoes, pasta, or rice. Serve immediately.

(SERVES 4)

½ cup of extra virgin olive oil

2 tablespoons of unsalted butter

½ cup of Dijon mustard

2 racks of lamb *(frenched)*

1 tablespoon of seasoned salt

1 tablespoon of black pepper

4 cloves of garlic

1 tablespoon of fresh rosemary
(coarsely chopped)

½ tablespoon of fresh thyme flakes

¼ cup of Worcestershire sauce

¼ cup of low sodium soy sauce

CHAMPAGNE **CHICKEN**

DIRECTIONS

In a large bowl, combine the flour, salt, pepper, and garlic powder. Place a large skillet on the stove and preheat over medium high. Add the butter and olive oil to the pan. Place the chicken in the flour and coat well. Shake off the excess flour and immediately place the chicken in the pan. Sauté the chicken for 3 minutes; add the mushrooms, scallions, and thyme to the pan. Turn the chicken over and add the chicken broth and white wine. Continue to cook for 2 minutes. Add the cream to the pan and reduce the heat to simmer for an additional 4 minutes. Place the chicken on a platter or serving plate. Spoon the sauce over the chicken and enjoy. Wild rice is an excellent side dish for this recipe.

(SERVES 6)

1 ½ cups of all-purpose flour

1 tablespoon of seasoned salt

1 tablespoon of coarse black pepper

1 ½ tablespoons of garlic powder

2 tablespoons of butter

2 tablespoons of extra virgin olive oil

6 boneless skinless chicken cutlets

4-6 baby Bella or white mushrooms

3 tablespoons of chopped scallions

3 teaspoons of dry thyme flakes

⅓ cup of chicken broth

¼ cup of white cooking wine

¼ cup of heavy cream

NO GRAVY **MASH**

DIRECTIONS

Place the potatoes in a large saucepan. Use just enough chicken broth to cover the potatoes. Bring the potatoes to a boil and continue to cook until the potatoes break when pierced with a fork.

Drain the potatoes. Add the butter and sour cream to the potatoes. Use a potato masher to mash the potatoes, butter and sour cream. Add the garlic powder, onion powder, thyme, pepper and salt. Mix well with a wire whip. Add the half and half and mix until smooth.

Serve with your favorite roast or meal.

(SERVES 6)

3 ½ pounds of white potatoes
(peeled and quartered)

8 cups of chicken broth

2 sticks of salted butter
(softened at room temperature)

1 cup of sour cream

2 tablespoons of minced garlic or granulated garlic powder

2 tablespoons of onion powder

1 tablespoon of dried thyme

3 teaspoons of white pepper

3 teaspoons of salt

2 cups of half and half

CHICKEN & CORN CHOWDER

DIRECTIONS

(SERVES 6-8)

Preheat a medium to large pot on the stove over medium high heat. Add the olive oil to the pot. Place the chicken in the pot and began to sauté the chicken for about 1 minute. Add the onion, celery, garlic, thyme, rosemary, potatoes, and corn. Sauté the ingredients for about 4 minutes, add the rotisserie seasoning, seasoned salt, and chicken broth. Bring the mixture to a boil. Cover the pot and reduce heat to simmer for about 20 minutes. Stir in the heavy cream and half and half. Allow the chowder to continue to cook for an additional 10 minutes on low heat.

Place a nonstick skillet on the stove over medium high heat. Place the butter in the skillet and allow it to get hot, but not smoking. Stir the flour into the butter. Continue to stir while the butter and flour thickens. This is called a roux. Return the chowder to a boil. While the chowder is boiling, add the flour and butter mixture to the chowder. Stir well. This will thicken the chowder. Continue to cook for about 4 additional minutes. Ladle the chowder into bowls, garnish with flat leaf parsley and serve immediately.

¼ cup of extra virgin olive oil

1 pound of boneless skinless chicken breast
(diced, wash the chicken and pat it dry)

1 pound of chicken thighs
(diced, wash the chicken and pat it dry)

1 medium onion *(small chopped)*

2 celery stalks *(small diced)*

4 cloves of garlic *(diced)*

1 tablespoon of fresh thyme leaves

1 tablespoon of fresh rosemary leaves

3 medium potatoes *(peeled and diced)*

1 tablespoon of coarse black pepper

2 cups of whole kernel corn *(frozen is ok as well)*

2 tablespoons of rotisserie seasoning

1 tablespoon of seasoned salt

6 cups of low sodium chicken broth

1 ½ cups of heavy cream

1 ½ cups of half and half

½ cup of unsalted melted butter

½ cup of all-purpose flour

3 tablespoons of flat leaf parsley *(garnish)*

MY FRIED
CABBAGE RECIPE

MY SISTER TRICIA CRAVES this dish way too much. I've also come to realize it's a favorite of several of the celebrity families that I've cooked for over the years. To tell the truth, I love it myself. It's a simple recipe with a lot of ingredient options that can be added to enhance the flavor and sweetness of your cabbage. My Aunt Bette loves to add red and green bell peppers. So, if it's for your favorite Sunday meal or an excellent addition to a corn beef recipe, this cabbage will knock your socks off and cause the flavors dance on your tongue!

(SERVES 4)

1 head of cabbage *(not the red variety)*
(shredded or chopped with the core removed)

3 tablespoons of butter

2 strips of turkey bacon

1 medium onion *(chopped)*

1 tablespoon of minced garlic

1 pinch of crushed red pepper flakes

2 teaspoons of sugar

2 cups of chicken broth

2 teaspoons of baking soda

DIRECTIONS

Wash the cabbage well. Shred or chop the cabbage and set aside. Preheat a large skillet or medium pot on the stove over medium high. Place the butter, bacon, onion, garlic, and crushed pepper flakes in the pan. Sauté the bacon mixture until the bacon is done. Place the cabbage in the pan and mix well. Cover the pan and allow the cabbage to become tender (about 4 minutes).

Add the sugar, chicken broth and baking soda. Mix well and continue to cook for an additional 2 minutes. Serve immediately.

THEA'S **GARDEN**

THIS IS A REALLY SIMPLE vegetable dish that can be served as a side or a complete meal for the vegetable lover. A dear friend of mine was on a fast eating nothing but fruit and vegetables. I wanted to come up with something that can be simple to prepare but also full of flavor. Besides, a dish like this is very beneficial for those who really want something light and quick. This can be prepared ahead of time and taken with you for a healthy snack. I promise you, if you heat this up and sit in your cubicle at work, you're going to cause a commotion from the smell alone. Did I mention that it's healthy?

DIRECTIONS

Place a large skillet on the stove and preheat over medium high. Add the olive oil and butter to the pan. Once the butter melts, add the carrots, zucchini, squash, and broccoli. Sauté the vegetables for 2 minutes, add the leeks, mushrooms, bokchoy, and bell pepper. Continue to cook for 1 minute. Add the remaining ingredients. Cook for an additional minute. Garnish with fresh rosemary and serve immediately.

(SERVES 4)

2 tablespoons of extra virgin olive oil

1 tablespoon of unsalted butter

2 large carrots *(diced)*

1 large zucchini *(large diced)*

1 large summer squash *(large diced)*

2 cups of broccoli crowns

2 medium leek stalks *(washed well & sliced)*

4 large mushrooms *(quartered)*

1 large portabella mushroom *(sliced)*

3 baby bokchoy *(diced)*

1 large red bell pepper *(diced)*

1 tablespoon of dried thyme

1 tablespoon of dried basil

1 tablespoon of garlic powder

1 tablespoon of coarse black pepper

½ tablespoon of seasoned salt

1 tablespoon of Mrs.Dash table blend

2 tablespoons of Worcestershire sauce

2 tablespoons of low sodium soy sauce

Fresh rosemary for *(garnish)*

BACON &
TOMATO SALSA

DIRECTIONS

Combine the vinegar, sugar, and salt in a plastic mixing bowl. Mix well until the sugar is completely dissolved. Add the basil and garlic. Give it a quick stir.

Place a small skillet on medium high heat. Add the bacon and shallot to the pan and cook until the bacon is completely done. Do not drain the oil from the bacon. Add the bacon and shallot mixture to the vinegar. Stir well. Add the diced tomatoes. Mix well. Cover and refrigerate until ready for use.

(SERVES 2)

¼ cup of red wine vinegar

1 tablespoon of sugar

Dash of salt

½ tablespoon of chopped basil

2 teaspoons of minced garlic

2 strips of bacon *(sliced)*

1 small shallot *(chopped)*

3 small plum tomatoes *(diced)*

NOTE: THIS DISH WILL TASTE GREAT OVER FRENCH BREAD

ROSEMARY AND
PARMESAN REDS

DIRECTIONS

Place the potatoes in a medium size pot. Add just enough water to cover the potatoes. Place the pot over high heat. Bring the potatoes to a boil and cook until they are fork tender. While the potatoes are cooking, combine in a large mixing bowl the olive oil, butter, paprika, garlic, seasoned salt, black pepper, rosemary, and Parmesan cheese. Mix well.

Once the potatoes are tender to the touch, drain the potatoes in a strainer. Toss the potatoes in with the olive oil seasoning. Mix well.

Coat a casserole dish or cookie sheet with nonstick spray. Add the potatoes to the pan and distribute evenly. Place the potatoes in the oven and bake for 25 minutes. Serve with your favorite meal as a wonderful side dish. Enjoy!

(SERVES 4)

1 pound of red potatoes *(quartered)*

½ cup of olive oil

½ cup of melted butter

1½ tablespoons of paprika

2 teaspoons of dry thyme

3 tablespoons of granulated garlic

1 ½ tablespoons of seasoned salt

2 teaspoons of coarse black pepper

2 tablespoons fresh rosemary *(chopped)*

¼ cup of grated Parmesan cheese

PREHEAT the oven to 450 degrees.

PEAR
POTATO

HAVE YOU EVER ASKED yourself, "What do I do with these leftover mashed potatoes?" I can recall my days at the Benvenue Country Club in Rocky Mount, North Carolina, where a very talented executive chef by the name of Larry Kennedy came up with a creative item to accompany an already exciting plate. He called it "The Pear Potato." It looked good but tasted even better. It's not a dish one would make every day; however, I find it to be a lot of fun to prepare and it can oftentimes be served as a great ice-breaker when entertaining guests. Kids love to help with this dish. I use my **No Gravy Mash** recipe (page 113) for this creation.

(SERVINGS WILL VARY)

2 eggs *(beaten)*

1 cup of milk or water

4 cups of vegetable oil

3 cups of plain bread crumbs

4 cups of vegetable oil

4 cloves

4 bay leaves

DIRECTIONS

Follow my No Gravy Mash recipe. Cool the potatoes to room temperature if making this from fresh mashed potatoes. Use a serving spoon and measure approximately ½ to ¾ cup of potatoes. Form the potatoes into the shape of a pear. Set aside on a cookie sheet. In a large bowl combine the eggs and milk. Mix well.

Preheat the oil over medium high heat in a medium size pot. Do not overheat. Test the oil for readiness by dropping a pinch of bread crumbs into the oil. If it sizzles, then it's ready.

Gently place the potato into the egg and milk mixture. Lift the potato out of the egg mixture and carefully coat the potato in the bread crumbs while maintaining the shape of a pear. Place the potato onto a large serving spoon and carefully lower the potato into the oil. Allow the potato to brown evenly for about 15-20 seconds. Line a cookie sheet with paper towels and drain the potato well. Place 1 clove and 1 bay leaf into the top center of the potato to resemble a pear. Serve as soon as possible.

ROME'S
SAFFRON RICE

DIRECTIONS

Place a large pot on the stove and preheat over medium high. Add the olive oil, chicken, sausage, and ham. Cook for about 5 minutes. Add the scallops, onion, garlic, bell pepper, thyme, pepper, Creole seasoning and olives. Continue to cook for an additional 2 minutes.

Add the chicken broth, rice, and saffron. Bring the broth to a boil. Stir well. Cover the pot and reduce the heat to simmer. Cook for about 12 minutes. Add the shrimp and stir. Cover and continue to cook for an additional 6 minutes. Remove the pot from the heat. Let the rice stand for 5 minutes. Enjoy!

(SERVES 4)

1 tablespoon of extra virgin olive oil

1 large chicken breast *(diced)*

¼ pound of beef smoked sausage *(sliced)*

¼ cup of diced turkey ham

¼ pound of sea scallops

1 small onion *(chopped)*

1 tablespoon of minced garlic

1 green bell pepper *(chopped)*

2 teaspoons of thyme

2 teaspoons of coarse black pepper

1 tablespoon of Creole seasoning

½ cup of Spanish olives *(chopped)*

4 ½ cups of chicken broth

1 ½ cups of long grain rice

2 teaspoons of saffron threads

½ pound of size 16-20 shrimp

COUNTRY GREEN BEANS & POTATOES

DIRECTIONS

In a medium pot, add 6 cups of chicken broth and the smoked turkey leg. Bring the broth to a boil. Add the onion and red pepper flakes. Cover and reduce the heat to simmer. Cook for 1 hour.

Add the green beans. Return the heat to medium high and continue to cook for an additional 30 minutes. Add the potatoes and cook until the potatoes are fork tender.

(SERVES 4)

6 cups of chicken broth

1 small smoked turkey leg

1 small yellow onion *(chopped)*

3 teaspoons of crushed red pepper flakes

1 pound of fresh cut green beans

¼ pound of white potatoes
(peeled and cut)

SMOTHERED SQUASH

DIRECTIONS

Place a large skillet on the stove over medium high heat. Add the butter and melt. Add the squash and onions to the pan. Cook the squash for 5 minutes while stirring every few seconds to allow for even cooking.

Stir well. Add the seasoning. Cover and allow the steam to continue cooking the squash for an additional 5 minutes. Mix well and serve.

(SERVES 6)

3 sticks of salted butter

2 pounds of summer squash *(washed and all debris removed)*

2 yellow onions *(quartered)*

1 tablespoon of coarse black pepper

1 tablespoon of fresh chopped parsley

½ tablespoon of sugar

CHIPOTLE PORK CHOPS
WITH **SAUTÉED SPINACH**

DIRECTIONS

Preheat the oven to 400 degrees.

In a large container, combine all ingredients and mix well. Pour into a large roasting bag. Add the pork loin chops. Seal and refrigerate at least 1 hour or more. Place the roasting bag into a casserole dish. Place the dish in the oven for 1 hour or until the chops are tender.

Spinach retains a lot of water. This is the reason it wilts and reduces in volume tremendously. So when cooking spinach, remember you need at least 3/4 of a regular size bag for 1 person. If you love spinach the way my family does, I use at least 1 bag per person when preparing baby leaf spinach.

Combine the bacon, onion, and red pepper flakes. Cook on medium high heat until the bacon is done. Add the butter and when melted, add the remaining ingredients. Continue tossing until spinach is done.

(SERVES 4)

8 bone-in pork loin chops
  (washed and patted dry)

Juice of 2 limes

4 garlic cloves

¼ cup of olive oil

1 jalapeño pepper
  (seeds removed, cored, chopped)

1 teaspoon of crushed red pepper flakes

3 teaspoons of cumin

¼ cup of cider vinegar

¼ cup of soy sauce

1 tablespoon of sugar

SAUTÉED SPINACH
TO SEASON SPINACH YOU WILL NEED THE FOLLOWING:

2 strips of thick-cut bacon
  *(turkey bacon is a great substitute,
  for a healthier choice)*

½ onion *(chopped)*

A pinch of crushed red pepper flakes

(INGREDIENTS CONTINUE ON NEXT PAGE)

DIRECTIONS (cont.)

It should take about 3 minutes once the spinach is in the pan. Arrange the spinach in the center of the plate. Add the pork chop. Spoon the broth over the pork chops and enjoy!

1 tablespoon of salted butter

1 tablespoon of garlic

¼ cup of white wine

¼ cup of chicken broth
(vegetable brothe can be substituted)

8 cups of baby leaf spinach

If you **love spinach** the way
MY FAMILY DOES,
I use at least
ONE BAG PER PERSON
when preparing **baby leaf spinach.**

DUCK
CHOWDER

DIRECTIONS

In a large Dutch oven, add the duck, butter, olive oil, and bacon. Sauté for about 5 minutes while stirring constantly. Add in the thyme, oregano, seasoned salt, white pepper, cayenne pepper, and bay leaf.

Add the celery, carrots, onion, corn and potatoes. Continue to cook for about 4 minutes while stirring constantly. Add the potatoes, chicken broth, and half and half. Bring to a boil. Cover and reduce the heat to simmer. Cook for 15 minutes. In a small bowl, combine the heavy cream with the flour.

Blend until smooth. Add the cream paste to the pot while stirring. Bring the pot back to a boil for about 3 minutes. Ladle the soup into the bowls. Top with the chopped scallions.

SERVE WITH TOAST POINTS OR GARLIC BREAD.

3 tablespoons of flour

1 cup of chopped scallions

(SERVES 6-8)

4 boneless, skinless duck breast
(washed and diced)

1 tablespoon of butter

1 tablespoon of olive oil

2 strips of bacon *(chopped)*

3 teaspoons of thyme

1 teaspoon of oregano

1 ½ teaspoons of seasoned salt

1 ½ teaspoons of white pepper

½ tablespoon of cayenne pepper

1 large bay leaf

¼ cup of celery *(chopped)*

½ cup of shredded carrots

1 medium onion *(chopped)*

1 cup of whole kernel corn *(frozen)*

5 medium white potatoes
(peeled and medium diced)

3 cups of chicken broth

2 cups of half and half

6 tablespoons of heavy cream

CURRIED
LAMB CHOPS

DIRECTIONS

Place a large skillet on the stove and warm over medium high heat. Season the lamb chops with salt, pepper, and curry powder. Pour the olive oil into the skillet. Immediately place the chops in the skillet and brown on both sides for about 3-4 minutes.

Note: Lamb chops are traditionally served medium rare. However, I prefer mine medium well. Cooking times will vary.

Remove the chops to a serving platter when desired temperature is reached. Add to the skillet the shallots, garlic, thyme, and diced tomatoes. Sauté the sauce for two minutes and then add the sherry, tomato juice, seasoned salt, cinnamon and sugar.

Continue to cook for an additional 2 minutes. Turn off the heat. Stir in each slice of butter until melted. Spoon the sauce over the chops and garnish with the mint leaves. This dish is excellent over rice!

(SERVES 4)

16 small lamb loin chops

1 tablespoon of salt

1 tablespoon of coarse black pepper

½ tablespoon of Indian curry powder

½ cup of extra virgin olive oil

½ cup of shallots *(chopped)*

2 tablespoons of garlic *(minced)*

1 teaspoon of thyme

1 ½ cups of tomatoes *(diced)*

¼ cup of dry sherry cooking wine

½ cup of tomato juice

½ tablespoon of seasoned salt

1 teaspoon of cinnamon

1 tablespoon of sugar

4 tablespoons of salted butter *(sliced & cold)*

8-10 mint leaves *(garnish)*

JOSHUA'S
BROWNED
STEWED CHICKEN

MY SON LOVES THIS RECIPE. As I've mentioned in the chapter pages, my father has played a key role in my children's life. They love to cook. Joshua loves good soups and stews. This one in particular is his absolute favorite. At least it was at the time we created this rendition of the Jamaican favorite.

I have to be careful with saying something is Joshua's favorite. The last time I said that, we were guests at the 700 Club. I was making a black bean and corn salsa. I made the comment that the salsa was one of my kid's favorite. Kristy Watts asked Joshua whether he liked it. He replied, "Not really." He threw me right under the bus. It was hilarious. Funny thing about it and the thing that makes it worse, is that right after the show, he was killing that dip.

The producer said to the rest of us as we were standing around after the show, "Look over there." My son not only was enjoying the dip like it was his last meal, but immediately asked could we take it back to the hotel with us. My son is a real comedian. Kids!

(SERVES 4)

1 whole chicken
  (washed and cut into eights)

2 tablespoons of coarse black pepper

1 ½ teaspoons of cayenne pepper

6 cloves of garlic *(crushed)*

2 tablespoons of seasoned salt

3 teaspoons of ground ginger

2 teaspoons of crushed red pepper flakes

4 sprigs of fresh thyme

1 ¼ cups of Worcestershire sauce

½ cup of soy sauce

½ cup of brown sugar

1 ½ cups of coconut oil

1 large carrot *(diced)*

1 large onion *(diced)*

3 whole white potatoes *(large diced)*

2 cups of chicken broth

3 tablespoons of tomato paste

DIRECTIONS

In a large bowl, place the chicken, black pepper, cayenne pepper, garlic, seasoned salt, ginger, pepper flakes, thyme, Worcestershire sauce, soy sauce, and brown sugar. Mix well. Cover and place in the refrigerator overnight. Remove the bowl from the refrigerator. In a large pot, heat the coconut oil on medium high. Once the oil is hot, place each piece of chicken in the oil. Brown the chicken on all sides (about 10 minutes). Add the carrot, onion, and potatoes. Mix well.

Add the chicken broth and tomato paste. Mix well. Continue stirring the chicken every 5 minutes or so. Cook the chicken until tender (about 40 minutes). Serve in a bowl over peas and rice. I hope you enjoy this as much as Joshua does.

I have to **be careful** with
SAYING SOMETHING IS
JOSHUA'S **FAVORITE.**

THE BEST BROILED CHICKEN EVER

I LOVE BAKED CHICKEN. However, I've learned that you can't eat everyone's. Far too often it's served overcooked and dry. You can almost call it chicken jerky. So I wanted to come up with something juicy, not overcooked and with plenty of flavor.

When I was in the U.S. Army, we had a pretty good recipe called Savory Baked Chicken. It was tasty but still missing something. I modified this dish and came up with what I believe to be "The best broiled chicken ever."

(SERVES 4)

1 whole fryer
  (washed well, cut into individual pieces)

1 cup of soy sauce

1 cup of Worcestershire sauce

1 tablespoon of cracked black pepper

¼ cup of fresh parsley *(chopped)*

¼ cup of light brown sugar

3 tablespoons of granulated garlic

1 tablespoon of dried thyme

½ cup of olive oil

1 cup of chicken broth for basting

DIRECTIONS

Preheat the oven to 425 degrees. Combine all the ingredients in a large glass or plastic bowl. Mix well. Add the chicken to the marinade. Allow the chicken to marinate for 30 minutes to 24 hours.

Place the chicken onto a sheet pan with sides. Place the pan in the oven and bake for 45 minutes. Baste the chicken with the broth after 30 minutes of cooking time. Remove the pan from the oven and place the chicken on a platter.

Use the natural pan gravy over rice or mashed potatoes.

GRILLED LIME CHICKEN
SKEWERS

DIRECTIONS

Combine all the seasonings in a large bowl and mix well. Add the chicken and marinate for about 2 hours. In the meantime, soak the wooden skewers in water for about 30 minutes to prevent charring.

Thread the chicken onto the skewers. Place the chicken skewers on the grill. Rotate every 5 minutes to allow for even cooking.

(SERVES 4-6)

4 large boneless, skinless chicken breasts, or 6 boneless, skinless chicken thighs *(cut into cubes or strips, washed & patted dry)*

6 wood skewers

½ cup rotisserie seasoning

Seasoned salt to taste

½ tablespoon of coarse black pepper

2 tablespoons of garlic *(minced)*

½ cup of lime juice

Zest of 1 lime

2 tablespoons of fresh chopped cilantro

½ cup of olive oil

GRILLED CORNISH HENS WITH
HONEY, ORANGE & NUT GLAZE

DIRECTIONS

Coat a sheet pan with nonstick spray. Place the hens on the pan. Generously rub the olive oil over the hens. In a large bowl, combine the paprika, seasoned salt, garlic, thyme, pepper, orange zest, and onion powder. Mix well. Season the hens with the dry rub. Place the hens on a preheated grill. Rotate hens often to avoid burning. In the meantime, prepare the glaze by placing a saucepan onto the stove over medium high heat. Place the butter in the pan and when melted, add the orange juice, nuts, honey, brown sugar, vanilla, and parsley. Bring the glaze to a boil. Stir well. Remove the pan from the stove. Add the orange liquor to the glaze and return the pan to the stove. Stir well. Reduce the heat and simmer the glaze until thickened (about 15 minutes). Use a pastry brush and apply the glaze to the hens. Remove the hens from the grill and serve.

(SERVES 3-6)

DRY RUB

3 Cornish game hens *(split and washed thoroughly)*

¼ cup of olive oil

2 tablespoons of paprika

1 tablespoon of seasoned salt

2 tablespoons of granulated garlic

1 tablespoon of dried thyme

1 tablespoon of black pepper

Zest of 1 orange

1 tablespoon of onion powder

GLAZE

1 stick of unsalted butter

1 cup of orange juice *(no pulp)*

½ cup of chopped pistachios

½ cup of pure honey

1 tablespoon of brown sugar

1 teaspoon of vanilla extract

1 tablespoon of chopped parsley

1 ounce of orange liquor

SOUPS, **SALADS** &DRESSINGS

BEEF, BARLEY & BOURBON SOUP

DIRECTIONS

In a 5-quart pot, add the olive oil and preheat over medium high. In the meantime, add the salt and pepper to the flour and mix well.

Coat the beef with the flour mixture. Sauté the beef until browned on all sides. Add the onions, rosemary, and thyme. Add the Worcestershire sauce and beef broth. Bring the soup to a boil.

Add the barley. Stir well. Lower the heat to medium. Cover and cook the soup for about 20 minutes. Add the bourbon and continue to cook for an additional 10 minutes. Spoon the soup into bowls. Garnish with fresh parsley leaves and serve.

(SERVINGS WILL VARY)

½ cup of olive oil

2 pounds of beef chuck tender *(small diced)*

½ cup of all-purpose flour

1 tablespoon of salt

1 tablespoon of coarse black pepper

2 medium onions *(chopped)*

2 tablespoons of fresh rosemary leaves

2 tablespoons of dry thyme flakes

½ cup of Worcestershire sauce

2 quarts of beef broth

2 cups of barley

1 ¼ cups of good bourbon

Fresh parsley leaves

NAVY BEAN SOUP

DIRECTIONS

In a medium size pot, combine the bacon, onion, garlic, thyme and bay leaf. Cook the bacon until done. Add the paprika, cayenne pepper, parsley and chicken broth. Bring the stock to a boil.

Add the beans. Allow the soup to return to a boil. Cover the pot, and reduce the beans to simmer for an hour. Stir occasionally. Once the beans are tender, remove the pot from the heat and serve immediately.

(SERVES 6)

2 cups of navy beans *((covered with water and soaked overnight))*

3 strips of thick-cut bacon

1 medium onion *(cut into strips)*

1 tablespoon of garlic *(minced)*

½ tablespoon of dried thyme

1 bay leaf

1 tablespoon of paprika

1 teaspoon of cayenne pepper

1 tablespoon of parsley *(chopped)*

12 cups of low sodium chicken broth

CURRIED APPLE & ONION SOUP

DIRECTIONS

Place a large skillet on the stove and preheat over medium high heat. Melt the butter in the pan. Place the onions and the apples in the pan. Cover the pan and allow the mixture to sweat for about 4 minutes or until the onions and apples are soft.

Sprinkle the curry powder over the onions and apples. Stir well. Simmer the mixture for about 2 minutes. Continue stirring for about 2 minutes, or curry will burn. Add the white pepper, chicken broth, heavy cream, half and half, and brown sugar.

Bring the soup to a boil. Cover and reduce the heat to simmer. Simmer for 10 minutes. Pour the soup into a blender or food processor. Blend until smooth, about 10-15 seconds.

Pour the soup into bowls. Top the soup with sour cream and enjoy.

(SERVES 2)

1 stick of unsalted butter

2 medium Vidalia onions
(thinly sliced)

2 Granny Smith apples
(peeled, cored, chopped)

1 tablespoon of Indian curry powder

1 teaspoon of white pepper

1 cup of chicken broth

1 cup of heavy cream

½ cup of half and half

1 tablespoon of brown sugar

2 tablespoons of sour cream

ITALIAN SAUSAGE & POTATO SOUP
WITH **PARMESAN GARLIC TOAST**

DIRECTIONS

Place a medium pot on the stove and warm over medium high. Add the sausage to the pot and brown for about 4 minutes. Add the oil, shallots, garlic, celery and potatoes.

Continue to cook for about 4 minutes. Add the thyme, oregano, basil and peas. Stir well. Add the soy sauce and chicken broth. Bring the soup to a boil. Cover the pot and reduce the heat to simmer. Once the potatoes are fork tender, the soup is ready. Ladle the soup into bowls and serve with Parmesan garlic toast.

Slice the baguette lengthwise and set aside. Combine the remaining ingredients. Use a pastry brush to apply the butter to the bread. Bake the bread at 350 degrees for about 5 minutes or until its golden brown. Serve it immediately with the soup.

(SERVES 4)

1 pound of ground Italian sausage

1 tablespoon of olive oil

2 small shallots *(chopped)*

2 cloves of garlic *(chopped)*

1 celery stalk *(chopped)*

2 small potatoes *(unpeeled, rinsed well, diced)*

2 teaspoons of thyme *(fresh)*

2 teaspoons of oregano *(fresh)*

2 teaspoons of basil *(fresh)*

½ cup of sweet peas

¼ cup of soy sauce

8 cups of chicken broth

PARMESAN GARLIC TOAST

I loaf of fresh baguette

½ cup of melted butter

1 tablespoon of chopped parsley

1 tablespoon of garlic powder

2 teaspoons of kosher salt

3 tablespoons of Parmesan cheese

BLACK BEAN SOUP

DIRECTIONS

Place a 6-quart pot on the stove and preheat over medium high. Place the sausage, olive oil, shallot, garlic, bell pepper, and thyme in the pot. Cook the sausage for 2 minutes.

Stir well. Add the cumin and cilantro. Pour in the beans and mix well. Add the lime juice and chicken broth. Bring the beans to a boil. Cover the pot, reduce the heat to low. Simmer for 30 minutes. Spoon the soup into bowls. Top with a dollop of sour cream and sliced scallions.

(SERVES 4)

¼ pound of smoked turkey sausage (sliced)

2 tablespoons of olive oil

1 large shallot (chopped)

2 cloves of garlic (minced)

½ red bell pepper (chopped)

2 teaspoons of dried thyme

½ tablespoon of ground cumin

1 tablespoon of cilantro (chopped)

2 cans of black beans (do not drain)

¼ cup of lime juice

4 cups of chicken broth

½ cup of sour cream

2 tablespoons of scallions (small sliced)

ROME'S
SOUTHWESTERN
SOUP

DIRECTIONS

Rub the bell peppers evenly with the olive oil and roast them over an open flame. (Gas stove or grill will work best). Char the peppers on all sides. Once the peppers are charred, place them in a bowl of ice water. Peel off the charred skin. Dice the peppers and set aside. In a large pot, place the chicken, sausage, onion and garlic; sauté for 10 minutes. Add the cilantro, corn, thyme, chili powder, cumin, rotisserie seasoning, pepper, broths, hot sauce, soy sauce, sherry, lime juice, and sugar. Bring the soup to a boil. Cover and reduce to simmer for an hour. Combine the cornstarch and water. Return the soup to a boil. Pour the cornstarch mixture into the soup while stirring at the same time. Stir well. Once the soup thickens slightly, remove the soup from the stove. Add the bell peppers and crab meat. Mix well. Serve immediately.

¼ cup of sugar

3 tablespoons of cornstarch
    & 4 tablespoons of water
    (mix together for a smooth paste)

1 pound of lump crab meat

(SERVINGS WILL VARY)

2 large red bell peppers

2 large green bell peppers

¼ cup of olive oil

1 pound of boneless skinless chicken breast *(diced)*

1 pound of ground Italian sausage

1 large onion *(diced)*

6 cloves of garlic *(minced)*

3 tablespoons of cilantro *(chopped)*

4 ears of sweet yellow corn *(off the cob)*

2 tablespoons of dried thyme

3 tablespoons of chili powder

3 tablespoons of cumin

2 tablespoons of rotisserie seasoning

1 tablespoons of black pepper

3 cups of chicken broth

3 cups of beef broth

¼ cup of hot sauce

¼ cup of soy sauce

¼ cup of dry sherry

¼ cup of lime juice

ORIENTAL
CHICKEN SALAD

DIRECTIONS

Combine the romaine and radicchio. Refrigerate until ready for use. Place a large skillet on the stove and preheat on medium high for about 5 minutes. Add the sesame oil to the skillet. Season the chicken breasts with the ginger, garlic powder, and black pepper.

Sauté the chicken breasts for about 4½ minutes on each side. (Cook a little longer if necessary, but do not overcook.) Add the sesame seeds on both sides while cooking the breasts. Once they are done, remove them from the pan and place on a cutting board. Allow the chicken to cool for about 5 minutes before slicing.

Remove the lettuce from the refrigerator and divide onto 2 plates. Place the chicken on top of the lettuce. Top the salad with almonds, orange segments, and chow Mein noodles.

(SERVES 2)

2 cups of fresh romaine lettuce
(washed and drained well)

½ cup of shredded radicchio
(washed and drained well)

1 ½ tablespoons of sesame oil

2 large boneless skinless chicken breasts
(washed and drained)

1 teaspoon of ginger powder

1 teaspoon of garlic powder

1 teaspoon of coarse black pepper

1 teaspoon of black sesame seeds

1 teaspoon of white sesame seeds

1 tablespoon of toasted sliced almond

1 cup of mandarin orange segments

½ cup of chow Mein noodles

HERBED
BEEF SALAD

DIRECTIONS

Rinse the spring mix salad and drain well. Add the cilantro to the salad mix. Place the salad in the refrigerator until ready for use. In a large Ziploc bag, combine the Worcestershire sauce, herbs, salt, garlic, and olive oil. Place the steak in the bag and seal it. Allow the steak to marinate for at least 30 minutes in the refrigerator.

Preheat your grill. Remove the steak from the marinade and allow it to drain. Discard the remaining sauce. Grill the steak until the desired temperature is reached. Remove the steak from the grill and place it on a cutting board.

Cool the steak for about 3 to 5 minutes. Slice the steak against the grain. Divide the lettuce between two plates. Arrange the steak on the lettuce. Garnish with the tomato, eggs, onion, and blue cheese. Serve immediately.

(SERVES 2)

2 cups of spring salad mix

3 tablespoons of fresh cilantro leaves

2 ½ tablespoons of Worcestershire sauce

1 tablespoon of fresh oregano *(chopped)*

1 tablespoon of fresh thyme *(chopped)*

1 tablespoon of fresh rosemary *(chopped)*

1 tablespoon of kosher salt

1 ½ tablespoons of garlic *(minced)*

2 ½ tablespoons of extra virgin olive oil

2 pounds of flank steak

1 steak tomato *(quartered)*

2 boiled eggs *(quartered)*

1 small red onion *(sliced)*

½ cup of crumbled blue cheese

HOT SALMON SALAD WITH HORSERADISH MUSTARD DRESSING

DIRECTIONS

Wash and drain the greens well and refrigerate until ready for use. Place a skillet on the stove and preheat on medium high. Add the butter and olive oil to the skillet. Season the fish with the bay seasoning, garlic, and black pepper. Immediately place the salmon in the pan top side down and cover with a tight fitting lid.

Cook for 3 minutes. Remove the cover and turn the fish over. Add lime juice, wine and capers. Continue to cook the salmon for an additional 5 minutes or until done. Divide and arrange the greens between 2 plates. Remove the salmon fillets from the skillet and place them onto the greens, spooning a few of the capers from the skillet onto the salmon.

Combine all the ingredients in a small bowl. Mix well with a wire whip. Spoon the sauce over the greens and salmon. Serve immediately.

(SERVES 2)

2 ½ cups of mixed field greens

1 tablespoon of butter

2 tablespoons of olive oil

2 salmon fillets *(6-8 ounce, washed & patted dry)*

2 tablespoons of old bay seasoning

2 teaspoons of garlic powder

2 teaspoons of cracked black pepper

Juice of 1 lime

½ cup of dry white cooking wine

1 tablespoon of capers

4 cherry tomatoes *(halved)*

HORSERADISH MUSTARD DRESSING

3 teaspoons of horseradish

¾ cup of champagne vinegar

2 tablespoons of Dijon mustard

1 teaspoon of garlic *(minced)*

Pinch of salt

Pinch of coarse black pepper

2 teaspoons of sugar

¼ cup of olive oil

HERB-CRUSTED GRILLED CHICKEN SALAD WITH BALSAMIC VINAIGRETTE

DIRECTIONS

Rinse the chicken breasts with cold water and pat dry with a paper towel. Season the breasts with the basil, rosemary, thyme, seasoned salt, and black pepper.

Place the chicken in the refrigerator until ready for use. Rinse the greens and drain well. Place the greens in the refrigerator until ready for use.

With the exception of the olive oil, combine all the ingredients in a bowl and mix well. While stirring with a wire whip, pour a steady stream of oil into the dressing. Mix well. Divide the vinaigrette in half. Use half the vinaigrette to marinate the chicken breast for about 15 minutes. Preheat the grill. Grill the chicken for 4 minutes on each side until done. Remove from the chicken from the grill and allow it to cool for about 4 minutes.

Cut the chicken into strips. Place the greens in a large bowl. Pour the remaining vinaigrette over the greens and toss well. Place the greens on a serving plate or platter. Top with the breasts.

I enjoy this salad with toppings such as quartered tomatoes, cheese, boiled eggs and turkey bacon bits. Try it; this is a real winner. It's healthy and very filling.

(SERVES 4)

4 boneless skinless chicken breasts

1 tablespoon of fresh basil (chopped)

1 tablespoon of fresh rosemary (chopped)

1 tablespoon of fresh thyme flakes

Seasoned salt to taste

½ tablespoon of coarse black pepper

6 cups of mixed salad greens

BALSAMIC VINAIGRETTE

1 cup of red wine vinegar

½ cup of sugar

4 tablespoons of garlic (chopped)

3 shallots (finely chopped)

6 tablespoons of Dijon mustard

8 tablespoons of balsamic vinegar

2 tablespoons of dry basil

2 teaspoons of salt

2 teaspoons of coarse black pepper

¼ cup of olive oil

MY FAVORITE
PASTA SALAD

DIRECTIONS

Bring a large pot of water to a boil. Add about a tablespoon of salt. Add the pasta to the water and stir well. Allow the pasta to cook for about 8 minutes. Under cold water, pour the pasta into a colander and rinse until cooled. Drain well. Add olive oil.

Pour the pasta into a large bowl. Season the pasta with seasoned salt, Italian seasoning, pepper, and garlic, olives, shallots, tomatoes, and Parmesan cheese. Toss the pasta well. Add the parmesan dressing and mix well. Refrigerate for at least 4 hours.

(SERVES 8-10)

1 ½ cups of rotini pasta

⅓ cup of olive oil

1½ tablespoons of seasoned salt

1½ tablespoons of Italian seasoning

½ tablespoon of coarse black pepper

2 tablespoons of garlic *(minced)*

¼ cup of green olives *(sliced)*

1 small can of ripe olives *(chopped)*

2 shallots *(minced)*

2 medium tomatoes *(diced)*

½ cup of Parmesan cheese

2 bottles of Parmesan dressing

8 PEPPER
VINAIGRETTE

DIRECTIONS

With the exception of the olive oil, place all the ingredients in a blender or food processer. Blend for about 20 seconds. With the blender running, add the olive oil in a steady stream. This will cause the dressing to emulsify. Pour the vinaigrette over your favorite greens or use it as an excellent marinade for chicken, beef or ribs.

1 medium yellow bell pepper *(minced)*

1 medium green bell pepper *(minced)*

1 small onion *(chopped)*

4 cloves of garlic *(crushed)*

1 Ancho chili pepper

1 serrano pepper

1 chipotle pepper

2 teaspoons of cracked black pepper

1 teaspoon of ground white pepper

1 teaspoon of cayenne pepper

1 tablespoon of caraway seeds

1 cup of red wine vinegar

¼ cup of balsamic vinegar

¾ cup of sugar

1 teaspoon of salt

3 tablespoons of Dijon mustard

¾ cup of extra virgin olive oil

GARLIC
&GINGER
DRESSING

DIRECTIONS

In a food processor, combine the vinegar, lemon juice, pepper flakes, shallot, garlic, ginger, thyme, and mustard, salt and pepper. Blend for about 20 seconds. While the machine is still running, slowly add the olive oil. Continue to blend for about 10 seconds. Refrigerate until ready for use.

¼ cup of white wine vinegar

2 tablespoons of lemon juice

1 teaspoon of crushed red pepper flakes

1 shallot *(minced)*

1 clove of garlic *(crushed)*

½ tablespoon of fresh ginger *(minced)*

1 teaspoon of dried thyme

2 tablespoons of Dijon mustard

Pinch of salt

Pinch of pepper

¼ cup of olive oil

SOUTHWESTERN
DRESSING

DIRECTIONS

Combine all the ingredients in a food processor or blender. Mix well for about 30 seconds.

¾ cup of red wine vinegar

Juice of 1 lime

2 small tomatoes *(diced, seeds removed)*

1 tablespoon of ground cumin

1 tablespoon of ground oregano

1 tablespoon of garlic *(minced)*

1 tablespoon of chili powder

2 teaspoons of paprika

¼ cup of sugar

2 tablespoons of fresh cilantro leaves

1 tablespoon of parsley *(chopped)*

¼ cup of extra virgin olive oil

ASIAN
SPECIAL
DRESSING

DIRECTIONS

Place all ingredients in a blender and mix well. Blend for about 20 seconds. Refrigerate until ready for use.

½ cup of rice wine vinegar

Juice of 2 limes

¼ cup of soy sauce

½ cup of brown sugar

1 tablespoon of garlic *(chopped)*

2 tablespoons of cilantro *(chopped)*

2 teaspoons of chili paste

1 tablespoon of sesame oil

CRANBERRY VINAIGRETTE

DIRECTIONS

Bring the water to a boil. Add the sugar and stir until totally dissolved. Add the cranberries and stir until thawed and well mixed. Pour the sauce into a blender. Add the mustard, garlic, salt and pepper. Blend for about 10 seconds. While the machine is running, add the grape seed oil. Refrigerate until ready for use.

1 cup of water

1 cup of sugar

½ cup of frozen cranberries

¼ cup of red wine vinegar

¼ cup of balsamic vinegar

2 tablespoons of Dijon mustard

2 teaspoons of garlic *(minced)*

Pinch of salt

Pinch of ground black pepper

¼ cup of grape seed oil

CHINESE
DIPPING SAUCE

DIRECTIONS

Combine all the ingredients in a small mixing bowl. Use a wire whip and mix well until the sugar is dissolved. Spoon the sauce over your favorite salad or use for dipping your favorite appetizer.

1 cup of rice wine vinegar

1 cup of low sodium soy sauce

2 teaspoons of crushed red pepper flakes

½ cup of sugar

1 tablespoon of scallions *(chopped)*

DESSERTS

JASMINE'S
POUND CAKE

AS YOU ALL KNOW, I started cooking at the age of 7, when I got up one morning and began making pancakes. It's amazing to sit back and watch my son and daughter follow my footsteps in the kitchen. I can remember my daughter making me a ham sandwich for the first time.

She put so much mayo on that sandwich I almost gagged. But I ate it anyway. It was my way of encouraging her. I guess it reminds me of that moment when my mother came into that kitchen and said, "Turn down the flame, it's too high." It served as a crossroad in my life, similar to that ham sandwich with far too much mayo on it.

I guess I should tell you that she was only 5 years old at the time. I'll reiterate the fact that my father has played a major role in teaching my children how to navigate the kitchen. One recipe that will always be a family favorite is this pound cake.

3 sticks of unsalted butter

1 cup of sour cream

3 cups of sugar

6 eggs

3 teaspoons of vanilla flavoring

3 cups of cake flour

½ tablespoon of baking powder

4 ounces of instant vanilla pudding

PREHEAT the oven to 300 degrees.

NOTE: DO NOT OPEN THE OVEN UNTIL THE CAKE IS FINISHED. ALLOW THE CAKE TO COOL FOR ABOUT 10 MINUTES BEFORE TRANSFERRING TO A CAKE PLATE.

DIRECTIONS

In a large mixing bowl, combine the butter, sour cream, and sugar. Use a hand mixer to blend well until creamy and smooth. Add and blend 1 egg at a time until well incorporated.

DIRECTIONS

Add the vanilla flavoring and mix well. Scrape down the sides of the bowl.

Sift together the flour, baking powder, and pudding. Add the flour mixture to the batter 1 cup at a time. Scrape the sides of the bowl after blending each cup.

Using a nonstick Bundt pan, pour the batter into the pan evenly all around. Place the pan into the oven and bake at 300 degrees for 2½ to 3 hours. Cooking times may vary slightly depending on your oven.

It's amazing to **sit back and watch**
MY SON & DAUGHTER FOLLOW
MY **FOOTSTEPS**
IN THE *KITCHEN.*

GINA'S VANILLA WAFER
POUND CAKE

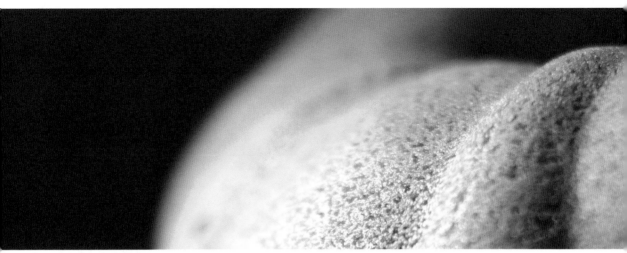

I'M NOT MUCH OF A BAKER, so whenever I go to Orlando, I have to get my cousin Gina to make me a Vanilla Wafer Pound Cake. According to her, she got it from her Grandmother Bernice. I don't care where it came from; I just know that it's one of my favorite cakes. It came out of my Aunt Freda's house, so it had to be good.

½ pound of unsalted butter *(2 sticks)*

2 cups of sugar

6 eggs

12 ounces of vanilla wafers
(crushed and ground)

1 teaspoon of baking powder

1 ½ cups of shredded coconut
(sweetend, 3 ½ ounces)

1 ½ cups of chopped pecans

DIRECTIONS

In a large mixing bowl, combine the butter, sugar, and eggs. Mix well with an electric hand mixer. Beat well until light and fluffy.

Combine the wafer crumbs and baking powder. Mix well. Add it to the butter mixture. Mix well. Add the coconut and pecans. Blend well.

Use a nonstick Bundt pan, or lightly grease and flour a Bundt pan. Pour the batter into the pan. Bake for 1 hour and 20 minutes.

Remove the pan from the oven. Cool for 30 minutes. Slice and enjoy.

PREHEAT the oven to 325 degrees.

CHOCOLATE CHIP
OATMEAL COOKIES

DIRECTIONS

In a large mixing bowl, cream the butter, brown sugar, and white sugar together. Beat in 1 egg at a time. Add the vanilla and mix well.

In a separate bowl, combine the flours and baking soda. Mix well. Use a wooden spoon to add the flour to the butter mixture. Mix well. Add the oats, walnuts, and chocolate chips. Stir well until all the ingredients are well incorporated.

Use a tablespoon to spoon the cookie dough onto an ungreased cookie sheet. Place in the oven on the middle rack. Bake the cookies for about 10-12 minutes. Remove the cookie sheet from the oven. Carefully use a spatula to take the cookies from the sheet and place them on a clean rack to cool.

(NUMBER WILL VARY)

2 sticks of unsalted butter

1 cup of firmly packed light brown sugar

½ cup of white sugar

2 eggs

3 tablespoons of vanilla flavoring

1 cup of cake flour

½ cup of all-purpose flour

½ teaspoon of baking soda

3 cups of uncooked oatmeal *(quick oats)*

1 cup of walnuts or pecans *(chopped)*

1 cup of semisweet chocolate chips

PREHEAT the oven to 325 degrees.

WANDA'S CARAMEL
APPLE SUPREME

IT WAS MOTHER'S DAY 2004. I was at my pastor's house in North Carolina. I'd just prepared dinner and he asked me, "Jerome, what's for dessert?" His beautiful wife said, "Yes, what's quick?" When I went into the kitchen, all I saw on the counter were three juicy red Delicious apples. This is what I came up with.

DIRECTIONS

Place a large metal bowl along with beaters from mixer in the freezer for about an hour. When ready to make the whipped cream, pour the cream into the bowl and beat with an electric mixer until the cream begins to form stiff peaks. Add the vanilla and sugar. Mix well, but do not over mix. Place a large skillet on the stove over medium high. Add the butter to the pan. When melted, add the pecans and apples. Cook for about 3 minutes. Stir constantly. Add the sherry and mace. Continue to cook for an additional 2 minutes. Set aside to cool.

(SERVES 6)

WHIPPED CREAM

1 cup of cold heavy whipping cream

1 teaspoon of vanilla

3 tablespoons of powdered sugar
(confectioners)

APPLE FILLIING

4 tablespoons of unsalted butter

3 tablespoons of pecans *(chopped)*

3 red Delicious apples *(large diced)*

4 ounces of sherry cooking wine

3 teaspoons of ground mace

QUICK CARAMEL

½ stick of unsalted butter

½ cup of light brown sugar

1 cup of sweetened condensed milk

GARNISH

1 fresh strawberry, raspberry, blackberry

6 mint leaves

DIRECTIONS (cont.)

To prepare the quick caramel, place a small pot on the stove on medium high. Add the butter and brown sugar. Mix until smooth. Add the milk and combine until mixed well. Place the whipped cream at the bottom of a cocktail glass.

Add the apple filling and then the caramel. Repeat until the glass is filled. Add the berries and mint as a garnish. Refrigerate until ready to serve.

PEACHES
A MILLION
PARFAIT

I MUST ADMIT when I think about the term "Peachy Keen," my father immediately comes to mind. He makes one of the best peach cobblers I've ever tasted. However, due to our ongoing cooking battle, I could never tell him that. He'd never let me live it down. So I came up with a gourmet peach recipe, if you will. It's an excellent item for something quick and entertaining. It's great and can be prepared ahead of time.

DIRECTIONS

Place the martini glasses in the refrigerator to chill. Place a metal mixing bowl with beaters from mixer in the freezer for about an hour.

(SERVES 4)

6 wide-rim martini glasses

3 fresh peaches *(pitted, peeled, and quartered)*

2 cups of sparkling Moscato wine

2 cans of quartered peaches in heavy syrup

3 teaspoons of cinnamon

1 teaspoon of nutmeg

2 tablespoons of sugar

1 cup of heavy whipping cream

2 teaspoons of vanilla extract

¼ cup of powdered sugar

4 fresh mint leaves *(garnish)*

Soak the fresh peaches in the Moscato wine and place in the refrigerator until ready for use. Place a small pot on the stove over medium high heat. Drain the juice from the canned peaches into the pot. Set the canned peaches aside. Add the cinnamon, nutmeg, and sugar. Bring the sauce to a simmer. Cook the sauce for about 10 minutes or until it thickens. Remove the sauce from the stove and cool at room temperature. Spoon the canned peaches into the sauce. In the meantime, while the sauce cools, remove the mixing bowl and beaters from the freezer. Pour the cream and vanilla into the bowl. Mix at a high speed until peaks begin to form. Add the powdered sugar and continue to whip until combined well.

Spoon the chilled peach mixture into the martini glasses. Top the peaches with the whipped cream. Garnish the parfait with 1 peach quarter and a mint leaf on top of the whipped cream.